IDEALS and ILLUSIONS

https://anamcara-press.com/the-write-bridge-zine/
Published biannually
Subscriptions: https://anamcara-press.com/subscribe-to-the-journal/
Cover Artword by
Book design by Maureen Carroll
Editors Maureen Carroll and Amber Fraley
Arial, Tomarik, Lato, Professor Minty
Printed in the United States of America.

Book description: 2025 Journal anthology

This periodical is devoted to literature in a broad sense, publishing short stories, poetry, plays, and essays, along with book reviews, biographical profiles of authors, interviews and occasional letters. The essays in this journal are works of creative nonfiction. The fiction in this journal are products of the author's imaginations or are used fictitiously and are not to be construed as real. Any resemblance to actual events, locales, organizations or persons, living or dead, is entirely coincidental.

Published by
ANAMCARA PRESS LLC
P.O. Box 442072, Lawrence, KS 66044
https://anamcara-press.com

Ordering Information: Quantity sales. Special discounts are available on quantity purchases for libraries, bookstores, and others. For details, contact the publisher at the address above.

CATALOGING DATA:
THE WRITE BRIDGE JOURNAL / Ideals and Illusions / Issue 8: Summer 2025
[edited by] Maureen Carroll [and] Amber Fraley

ISBN-13: 978-1-960462-63-3

ISSN: Pending
LCO010000 LITERARY COLLECTIONS / Essays
LCO020000 LITERARY COLLECTIONS / Interviews
HUM003000 HUMOR / Form / Essays
BIO026000 BIOGRAPHY & AUTOBIOGRAPHY / Personal Memoirs

"I really don't know life at all."
Line from "Both Sides Now"
—Joni Mitchel.

ANAMCARA
PRESS
LAWRENCE, KANSAS

SMALL PUBLISHER, BIG VOICES.

THE WRITE BRIDGE

| *MIND THE GAP* |

A Biannual Literary Journal

SELECT WORKS OF NON-FICTION, POETRY, FICTION & ART

ISSUE #8; SUMMER 2025

IDEALS and ILLUSIONS

Anamcara Press LLC | Lawrence, Kansas

PREVIOUS ISSUES OF THE WRITE BRIDGE

THE WRITE BRIDGE | MIND THE GAP | WINTER 2023/24
JOURNAL ISSUE #7
Theme: Grief and Comfort

THE WRITE BRIDGE | MIND THE GAP | WINTER 2023/24
JOURNAL ISSUE #6
Theme: Solitude and Solidarity

THE WRITE BRIDGE | MIND THE GAP | SUMMER 2023
JOURNAL ISSUE #5
Theme: Perilous and Playful

THE WRITE BRIDGE | MIND THE GAP | FALL 2022
JOURNAL ISSUE #4
Theme: Fortitude and Pusillanimity

THE WRITE BRIDGE | MIND THE GAP | SPRING 2022
JOURNAL ISSUE #3
Theme: Heartbreak and Desire

THE WRITE BRIDGE | MIND THE GAP | FALL 2021
JOURNAL ISSUE #2
Theme: Isolation and Emergence

THE WRITE BRIDGE | MIND THE GAP | SPRING 2021
JOURNAL ISSUE #1
Authors explore the topic of inclusion, and offer up some pandemic prose

WELCOME TO
THE WRITE BRIDGE JOURNAL

The Write Bridge presents two opposing ideas for creators and readers to delve into—seriously or in fun—in order stretch our imaginations.

In each edition, readers are encouraged to “mind the gap” as writers and artists explore topics that broaden our thinking and help us move beyond boundaries.

In a 1936 *Esquire* article entitled “The Crack Up,” author F. Scott Fitzgerald wrote:

> *“Before I go on with this short history, let me make a general observation—the test of a first-rate intelligence is the ability to hold two opposed ideas in the mind at the same time, and still retain the ability to function. One should, for example, be able to see that things are hopeless and yet be determined to make them otherwise. This philosophy fitted on to my early adult life, when I saw the improbable, the implausible, often the ‘impossible,’ come true.”*

We hope the themes for *The Write Bridge* Journal **Summer 2025 edition, *Ideals and Illusions*,** will offer lessons and comic relief on our human shortcomings and aspirations.

COVER ART
TIFFANY MAGNOLIAS AND IRISES
MARSENE FELDT

THE WRITE BRIDGE JOURNAL STAFF

The Write Bridge Literary Journal was created by Maureen "Micki" Carroll and Anamcara Press in 2021 in celebration of art and community, and in support of authors and artists in their creative endeavors.

Carroll is a writer, educator, graphic designer, and all around cat herder. Her first book, *A Wyoming Cowboy in Hitler's Germany* combines war era correspondence and 70 year old photographs to depict an age of heroism and innocence. *The Tree Who Walked Through Time* was published in collaboration with 17 artists, including crop artist Stan Herd. She is also the author of the middle-grade series, Jo & the School's Out Squad. Carroll Chairs the Kansas Authors Club District #2 in Lawrence.

Assistant Editor and Publicist, Amber Fraley is your typical Gen Xer suburban Kansas wife and mom of one who grew up a book nerd in a dysfunctional family and now writes about those experiences as hilarious therapy. She's the author of the humorous essay collection *From Kansas, Not Dorothy*, and the viral essay "Gen X Will Not Go Quietly," as well as numerous human interest articles. Amber loves Kansas with all her heart, is frequently awkward in public, and desperately wishes to see a tornado and live to tell the tale.

CONTRIBUTING VISUAL ARTISTS

CATHY MARTIN is a mixed-media artist who lives and works on ten acres of woodland and meadow in the rolling hills of beautiful NE Kansas. Surrounded by the rich color and tapestry of the Colorado mountains and Iowa farmlands in her youth, landscapes are her specialty, and Cathy enjoys adding various wildlife into many of her paintings.

MARSENE FELDT is a native Kansan who taught art for over 30 years before retiring from education. Now, as a self-proclaimed empty nester and feral housewife, she now works at illustrating and writing children's books. She enjoys gardening (plants and rocks), cooking, creating, reading, and traveling (especially if it involves trees, rocks, or beaches).

BOBBIE LYN POWELL attended KU and stayed in Lawrence KS for 17 years creating, showing, and selling mixed media art, children book illustrations, drawings, and paintings. A member of art co-op groups Dot Dot Dot and Quintessential 5, Bobbie has had shows in Kansas City and Lawrence. She's done multiple commission projects including a solo show at the Great Plains Nature Center, painted two large outdoor murals and worked on children's book illustrations. Bobbie has painted murals in Ark City KS, Lawrence KS, Wichita KS, Anthony KS, and Kiowa KS. She is currently working on illustrating three books, one tattoo design, and one commission painting for a private residence.

KENT SMITH (SMITTY) is a dimension-jumping illustrator, designer, sculptor, teacher, problem-maker, problem-solver, and magic-man sharing grand visions from afar. His work can be found on Star Wars toys, Free State beer labels, custom masks, huge woodblocks prints, giant festival sculptures and tiny trading cards.

Kent also celebrates teaching in the Design Department at the University of Kansas, as well as working with the Lawrence Arts Center, VanGo, Percolator and other fine organizations.

BARBARA WATERMAN-PETERS, (BFA, Washburn University, MFA, Kansas State University, Honorary Doctor of Fine Arts, Washburn University) taught at Washburn and Kansas State Universities as well as for Lassen Community College in California. She has received a Certificate of Recognition for Outstanding Achievement from the State of Kansas and the Monroe Award from the Washburn University Alumni Association. In 2011 she was awarded the ARTY for Distinguished Visual Artist from ARTS Connect in Topeka. Her work has been included in more than 300 solo, group and juried exhibits. She is represented by several galleries, Jones in Kansas City, SNW in Manhattan, and Beauchamp in Topeka. She owns STUDIO 831 in the North Topeka Arts & Entertainment District (NOTO).

CONTRIBUTING AUTHORS

Keri Ault
Will Averill
Boyd Bauman
Annette Hope Billings
Julie Ann Baker Brin
M. Carroll
Hannah Corynne Caycedo
Louis Copt
Iris Craver
Brian Daldorph
T.A. Dugan
Amber Fraley
Beth Gulley
Tasha Haas
Marilyn Hope Lake, Ph.D.
J.A. McGovern
Kerry Moyer
Dan Nagengast
Peg Nichols
Kevin Rabas
Kathy Roberts
Bruce Rolfe
Lesa F. Roberts
Ralvell Rogers
Kathy Roberts
Jesse Scott
Connlyn Sinclair
Craig Sweets
Chuck Warner
Barbara Waterman-Peters

With Special Thanks to:

Will Averil & Kent Smith
and
Ralvell Rogers

Our mission is to spark wonder. *The Write Bridge* is published twice a year and features powerful poetry, short fiction, and creative nonfiction, as well as interviews with influential authors and artists..

Contents

Introduction:
STRIVING FOR PERFECTION

The 'Ideal' is the standard by which we judge things, from circles, to sunrises, to people. It is unchanging perfection of the highest order. We inheritors of Platonic thinking understand the 'Ideal' is something we can aspire to, but never achieve.

We can create only flawed imitations of the 'Ideal.' The ideal song, book, or marriage doesn't exist. Perfection is just a shadow on the wall for mere mortals. This is because the 'Ideal' abides in a different reality—one that is eternal, perfect, and unchanging. Our reality is fleeting, flawed, and fluid.

As a writer, I think it is important to acknowledge the illusion of believing you can reach the 'Ideal.' I don't mean to say you shouldn't strive for perfection. But without giving a nod to your limitations, you might spin your wheels—fool yourself into thinking you *can* create the 'Ideal.'

It is what keeps us from moving on to the next project. It is what keeps us endlessly editing. Or worse, it is why we dropped those thoughts and dreams into a drawer years ago and never pulled them back out. We knew, consciously or unconsciously, we would never reach the 'Ideal' and gave up.

A Navaho (Diné) weaving tradition provides a great solution for our stalwart striving for the 'Ideal.' They weave a mistake into the blanket, knowing there will be no perfect blankets. Where the mistake is woven is where the bad juju comes out—releasing the desire for perfection that prevents forward motion. (My interpretation.)

The People call this a "spirit line" or "weaver's path," it is a deliberate flaw. A weaver will start from the center and work out, making a thin line or small break in the border pattern. They believe it provides a path for the spirit of the weaver to exit once the weaving is complete. Without it, the weaver's soul might remain trapped in the work. (I've known some writers who have been trapped in the work.)

Like Plato, Navaho weavers acknowledge that perfection lies beyond human creation and belongs to the realm of the divine. The Navajo "spirit line" is a gesture of respect. In the Navajo view, beauty *includes* imperfection because life itself is imperfect.

It is with this understanding we offer the 8th edition of The Write Bridge journal: *Ideals and Illusions.* The following articles, poems, stories, and plays demonstrate the power of ideals and illusions to compel us to act—or to refrain from taking action; to urge us toward or away from our aspirations.

When we are young, idealizing things comes easy. As Amber Fraley describes in *Making Peace with the Wizard of Oz.*

ESCAPE, MAUREEN CARROLL

"Now that I'm older, I can see the backgrounds are clearly matte paintings, and every scene is obviously filmed on studio stages. But that's not how I saw it as a kid. As a kid, Oz the movie might as well have been made with high-tech computer graphics. I bought it completely."

When we are older and wiser, our desire for perfection can leave us tongue-tied. Jesse Scott and Keri Ault wonder in *You Can't Get Rid Of Me: An adopted son's search for family*—what do you say when you meet your birth mother for the first time?

"I'm trying to figure out what I should call her. 'Donna' seems too casual, like we're pals or something. 'Mom' doesn't feel right either. Not yet. In my head I'm calling her 'Mom Donna' because my own mother is the person I call 'Mom.' So far I've gotten away with not calling her anything to her face. Maybe I should calm down and realize I'm only four hours into this thing, and that some of this stuff will work itself out."

Our ideals seem to drive our illusions. We want a perfect family, so we struggle with what to say. Or we seek a perfect friendship, and fall victim to scammers.

Scamming—creating illusions—starts when we are young, too. We call it pranking. As Peg Nichols admits in *Idle Algorithms,* Boredom is responsible for a lot of pranks:

"In the early evening hours supervision would be light and the lack of activity boring. I had a way to amuse myself that was never discovered and for which I was never fired. I could cause the telephones to ring in two houses at the same time. At each house someone would take the phone from the wall, thinking that the other party had called. ... Often the dialogues were quite entertaining. "You called?" "No, you called."

This is amusing because part of humor comes from being tricked or seeing others fooled by their own imaginings.

Louis Copt in *No Peace In Greece!* admitted the humor of his illusions as an American traveler with high ideals:

> ***"Out of the fog emerges a lone man in a military box. His laughter slices through the wind. ...***
>
> ***"Is there a bus?"***
>
> ***His laughter is a bitter echo across the plain. "No bus," he grins. "You walk. Forty kilometers.'"***

Illusions are not always funny as they can easily turn into deceptions. Hope Lake admits in *Not An Accomplice* that in addition to joining her friend in tricking her friend's grandmother,

> ***"I was complicit in teenage crimes also. In Illinois, girls could buy and drink alcohol at the age of 18. Boys had to be 21. I bought many a six-pack or bottle of wine for parties, or for boys I liked, during the three years before it was legal for them to drink."***

We can reject ideals and deliberately choose the illusion. Like a teenager flipping-off authority, some illusions soothe like poison.

The biggest illusions are those we perpetrate upon ourselves. Kathy Roberts describes how everything in her life had become too much in *New York*:

> ***"Grocery shopping, staying sober until noon, watching TV, leaving the house ..."***

And yet she forced herself to go to a job interview in New York that was bound to burst her bubble.

As we age, still striving for the ideal, illusions cast long shadows. Chuck Warner warns in *The Truth Never Rhymes:*

Life has no perforated edges.

Annette Hope Billings, "Perforation"

One of the basic rules of the universe is that nothing is perfect. Perfection simply doesn't exist. Without imperfection, neither you nor I would exist.

—Stephen Hawking

"Histories and Memoirs are flawed by the writer's memory and biases. Add to that, now that I am in my seventies and many of those events in my life occurred a long time ago, well, my memory isn't what it used to be."

The contributing authors express both our striving for our ideals and our falling victim to our illusions, seriously and humorously, in this edition of The Write Bridge.

As poet Annette Hope Billings reminds us— "life has no perforated edges." So, if you're a creative type, consider building in a little flaw, just a small place to allow you to exit when the work is complete.

—Maureen (Micki) Carroll, Editor-in-chief

We at Anamcara Press offer our prayers and support to the courageous Ukrainians.

Etymology

The featured word for this issue's etymology review is:

ILLUSION

"Illusion consists either in perceiving a totally wrong object in place of the right one . . . or in investing the right object with the wrong attributes."

Latin: *illusiu* **"play, mock, jeer,"**

Old French: *illusion* **"deceit, a trick of the senses"**

English: *ludicrous* **"ridiculous, absurd"**

"A FALSE CONCEPTION OR IDEA"

Deceit "fraud, cheating, false dealing"

To deceive is to 'catch' or 'ensnare' someone. From 'de' and 'caapere' ('take' and 'seize'—the source of the English 'capture')

—caught, seduced, deluded, misled, beguiled, fooled, tricked, or duped

"By violence? no ... but by deceit and lies." —S. Williams (1794).

"jesting, trifling, frivolous"
"deception, delusion, fancy"

"Concealment of the truth in order to mislead."

Definitions from the *Compact Edition of the Oxford English Dictionary*, **Oxford University Press 1971, and** *Dictionary of Word Origins*, **John Ayto, Arcade Publishing 1990.**

ANIMALIA (HOMAGE), BARBARA WATERMAN PETERS

PART I:
ARTICLES & ESSAYS

WEAVING IT ALL TOGETHER

Featured essays submitted for the Summer 2025 edition of *The Write Bridge* include fond—and not so fond—memories of Kansas. Amber Fraley waxes eloquent on the virtues of *The Wizard of Oz*. While Randy Kidd, in *Fog*, reminds us *"Kansans know this kind of sky can quickly turn into the full-blown tornado that transports Dorothy and Toto into another world.*

Jesse Scott finds another world when he meets his birth family in, "Mom Donna." Dan Nagengast discovers his Sunday School teachers were hiding all the good stuff in "My Failed Religious Training." And Beth Gulley discovers her mother to be a very different person than she ever expected in "Ellen's Idol," and more.

We'd also like to acknowledge the passing of our dear friend Louis Copt, an amazing artist and man whom we've all lost far too soon. We are so glad we're able to share his words about hitchhiking from Greece to the former Yugoslavia in this issue.

WILL AVERILL

KENT SMITH

Interview With An Author/Artist Duo:

WILL AVERILL & KENT SMITH

— by Amber Fraley

Lawrence actor and writer Will Averill and artist Kent Smith are collaborating on a new book to be published in 2025 through Anamcara Press. *Day After the Wasteland* is a takeoff on T.S. Eliot's modernist narrative poem *The Waste Land*, except *Day After the Wasteland* is about Lawrence, Kansas.

Averill's epic poem is peppered with his famous sense of humor and illustrated by artist Kent Smith's lively drawings.

Will Averill

Amber Fraley: How did the idea for Day After the Wasteland come about?

Will Averill: I first encountered T.S. Eliot in college, and his work made no sense. I then encountered him in England, as he and I were both American expats, and his works started to make a lot more sense. When I came back from England, I was searching for a way to connect the importance of all the life lessons I'd learned there with my love for Lawrence, my hometown, and the result was this project. At first, it was just one second, and based on "March is the maddest month" being a funny play on Eliot's opening line. However, it was good and it stuck, so I kept building it. This piece took about five years to complete. Not all at once, but in parts.

AF: Where do you think your sense of humor comes from?

WA: I had a lot of amazing comic mentors, growing up in a theatre family. I watched Monty Python from a young age, which would ruin anybody. I also watched my parents do vaudeville at night for adults and children's shows that were funny during the day for kids. Each one had their places, but I have always loved and respected the healing and community-building power of laughter. My comic mentor was Dale Easton, a Topeka-based vaudevillian, who taught me about stillness, audience interaction, and taught me not to take myself or my work too seriously.

AF: People who know you know you have a background in theater—can you talk about how that informs your poetry?

WA: If theatre is a temporal physical expression of the human experience existing for that brief moment of performance, poetry, to my mind, is an aural and written expression. Words each come with their own meaning to two people: the audience and the author. Poetry explores the way in which those interpretations join, interact, and come in conflict with each other. I find poetry informs my dialogue and scene structure as much as my performative nature informs the narrative and drive of my poetry.

AF: What do you hope people get from Day After the Wasteland?

WA: I hope they laugh, think "did someone really take the time to do this?" and then over the coming weeks and months, look at Lawrence a little differently through the lens of the work's amazing, stripped-down illustrations of Lawrence, as well as by the poem's surprising and pop-culture ridden vision of a city forever stuck in flow—between modern and historic, between sports and arts, between underage bars and overpromised development. I hope it brings people laughter, hope, joy, and a fresh perspective on this amazing place.

AF: What's your philosophy about writing?

WA: As a kid I did it to impress adults, in my teens and did it to anger adults, in my college years and through my twenties I did it for the ladies, in my thirties I wrote to understand my twenties, in my forties I wrote to bring myself comfort in times of uncertainty and failure. So far, in my fifties, I'm writing because I feel compelled, as someone who believes in the good of humanity despite all available evidence, to be a beacon of what America can be, that of the values I was taught in my childhood - a place where free expression is encouraged, people's hopes and dreams are valued, and we remember that to be the strongest, we must be there for the weakest. I'd eventually like to make money at it.

AF: What's it been like collaborating with Kent?

WA: When I first thought about how to make this dream a reality, once I had the poem, I wanted so much for the illustrations to be done by Kent. His sketch class on Lawrence locations has been an inspiration to my own writing, and his mad genius chaotic brain, I knew would find a place for this project, because it is really a silly idea, when you think about it too much. I cannot tell you how amazing it has been to work with Kent. It gives the whole piece an amazing "Zine meets Penguin Classics" look that perfectly fits the text. He also has some of the best hair in the business. 10/10, would recommend partnering with Kent Smith anytime.

Kent Smith

AF: When did you know you wanted to be an artist?

KS: I was an art kid from the start. I loved comics and cartoons. I drew in the margins of all my assignments. Drawing was my "fidget spinner" and the only way I was able to sit still in class/church/meetings (it still is). As a kid, once I found out people got to be an artist as their job, it felt like I had just figured out a cheat code to life.

AF: Did you have any mentors along the way who influenced you?

KS: Yes! I was not able to conjure my magic from thin air. I was lucky enough to have some great guidance from some wise wizards along the way. I grew up with a family friend who was a freelance cartoonist named Tom Fisher. He was the first person to teach me to draw. He also steeped us in illustration, comics, movies and animation history. Besides drawing, he taught me how to tell a story. Later, in college, I was lucky enough to have Barry Fitzgerald and Dick Varney as professors. They taught me the value of creative process and how to seek and design successful creative solutions.

AF: What artists inform your work?

KS: I am inspired by a lot of different artists, eras, and genres. There is a thread that connects my work through fine artists like Alphonse Mucha, Egon Schiele, and Maxfield Parish; illustrators like Windsor McKay, Norman Rockwell, Rube Goldberg and JC Leyendecker; painters like John Berkey and James Gurney; as well as the work of many contemporary image makers like Kim Jung Gi, James Jean, Chris Visions, Jamie Hewlett and others. I am a sponge and find inspiration in most anything I look at. The trick is to play with something, remix it, and smash it together with other influences until it hopefully becomes something new.

AF: Do you have a ritual or a routine for making art?

I carry my sketchbook with me everywhere. I try to get into it as often as possible. It is a ritual based in experimentation and regular practice and it grounds. It isn't about making perfect work or "finished" images, but it does often end up leading me to new ideas for work. It allows me to play.

KS: What's your philosophy about art? Why do you make art?

I try to offer celebration of the mundane and an escape into fantasy and fun through my artwork. I love silly ideas and try to elevate them into something with depth. In my urban sketches I celebrate time and place and connect to the history found in these special structures around town.

AF: What's it been like collaborating with Will?

KS: Collaborating with Will has been easy, and he has been a great champion for the project. I was honored when he reached out about using drawings from my sketchbooks and it encouraged me to see this collection of Lawrence locations through new lenses and with new value. Seeing the drawings alongside Will's ridiculously smart reinterpretation of T.S. Eliot's work is the coolest.

WILL AVERILL is a writer, director, and nonprofit professional based in Lawrence, Kansas, with a background that bridges the arts and community work. A graduate of the University of Kansas with a degree in Theatre, Will has spent over two decades creating original works for stage, radio, and screen—often with a healthy dose of humor, heart, and the occasional puppet.

He co-founded Card Table Theatre, producers of The Victor Continental Show, a long-running sketch comedy and music revue beloved for its irreverence and sold-out audiences. Currently, he is the Chief Operating Officer at the Ballard Center in Lawrence, helping families in crisis and supporting early learning initiatives across Douglas County.

KENT SMITH (SMITTY) is a dimension-jumping illustrator, designer, sculptor, teacher, problem-maker, problem-solver, and magic-man sharing grand visions from afar. His work can be found on Star Wars toys, Free State beer labels, custom masks, huge woodblocks prints, giant festival sculptures and tiny trading cards.

Kent also celebrates teaching in the Design Department at the University of Kansas, as well as working with the Lawrence Arts Center, VanGo, Percolator and other fine organizations.

COMING SOON!

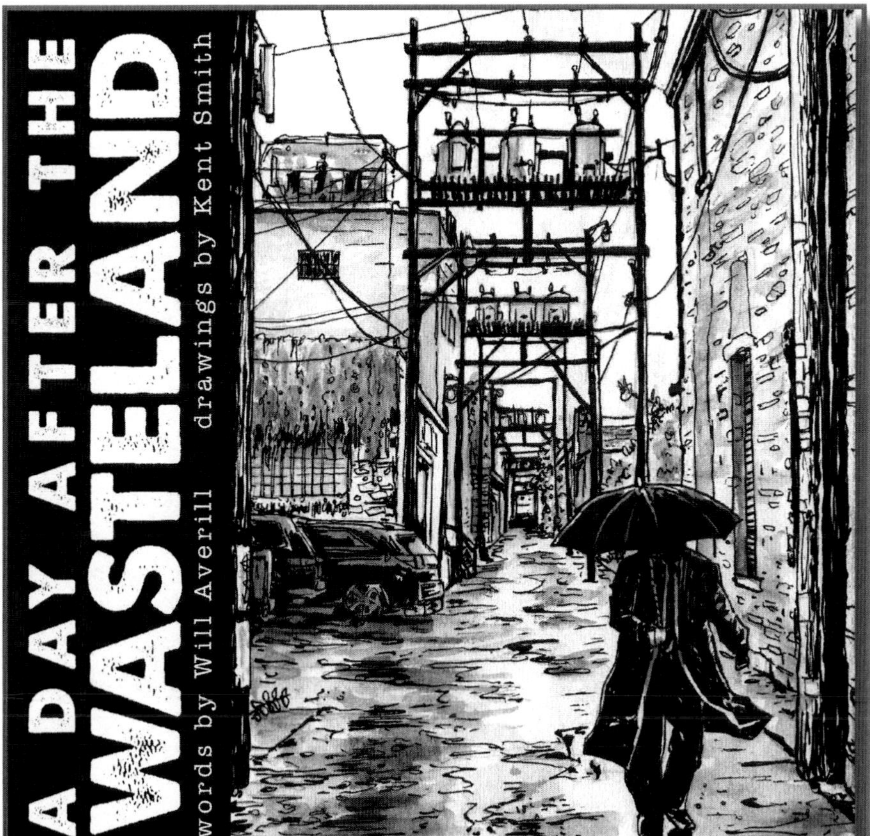

ARCHEBALDO THE GARDENER , MARSENE FELDT

Making Peace with *The Wizard of Oz*:

Amber Fraley

My first memory of watching the ***Wizard of Oz*** is a brief flash in my mind, lying on our 1970s gold velvet couch, watching Dorothy's gray house get sucked up into the sepia tornado. I was lying down because I'd had a hard day of playing and I was only four. I didn't really understand the movie I was watching, but somehow, I knew it was important. "Kansas" wasn't yet a concept for me, and my family was living in Tennessee at the time. That same year though, we'd move back to Kansas, the state where my parents were born—as well as four previous generations—the place from which all our people hailed.

Like the annual arrival of Easter, the special movie came to television in the spring of every year, and we never missed it, because in our house, as in many Kansas homes, it was treated like an event. *It's* Wizard of Oz *time again! Get the popcorn!* I'll probably go to my grave knowing there's a commercial break after the Cowardly Lion runs and jumps through the window of the Wizard's palace, shattering the glass.

When you're from Kansas, you're far more aware of this movie in daily life than your average American. Even though ninety percent of the movie doesn't even take place in Kansas, Kansas and the *Wizard of Oz* are inextricably linked.

For one thing, it's about the only thing people know to associate with Kansas. There used to be a time many Americans knew Kansas as the largest producer of wheat in the United States, because they were familiar with the phrases "Breadbasket of America," or "Wheat State." But no one knows those sayings anymore, and lots of people from outside of Kansas seem to think Kansas grows a lot of corn.

I've found many city dwellers assume anything growing in a field is "corn." However, corn is Kansas' second largest row crop, while Iowa is the top producer of corn in the US.

Sure, some people think of the Kansas City Chiefs, but the Chiefs are a Missouri team—Kansas City is one of those cities that straddles two states—and most of the fun stuff, of course, is in Missouri. (Yes, I know they are actually two cities, but around here we don't really treat them as such.)

Often the only tangible idea of Kansas other Americans have to grab onto is the film *The Wizard of Oz.* When you're from Kansas, and you leave Kansas, you will hear *Wizard of Oz* Comments.

"How's Toto?" People ask, chuckling to themselves, as though they're the first to think of it. Or, if you're female, they'll ask "Are you Dorothy?"

It gets old. ... At least, when you're in your teens and twenties and thirties, and things like that are annoying. Now that I'm in my forties I've made my peace with the *Wizard of Oz.*

When I was four, and for many years thereafter, I would be completely sucked into the wonderful world of Oz, buying every second of it. Now that I'm older, I can see the backgrounds are clearly matte paintings, and every scene is obviously filmed on studio stages. But that's not how I saw it as a kid. As a kid, *Oz* the movie might as well have been made with high-tech computer graphics. I bought it completely. (Okay, not the shiny plastic flowers in Munchkin Land. I wasn't a total idiot.)

I watched *The Wizard of Oz* again recently, and I was struck by how good the actors are, and how fun it is to listen to their charming Mid-Atlantic accents, which is the name for that haughty, almost British accent early American actors used. (Think Cary Grant and Katherine Hepburn.)

"No haht?" Dorothy and the Cowardly Lion ask the Tinman when he tells them the tinsmith created him without a heart. "No haht," he sighs.

Lovely.

Curious, I looked up the three guys who play the Scarecrow, the Tinman and the Cowardly lion—who also play the farmhands Hunk, Hickory and Zeke—whose real names are Ray Bolger, Jack Haley and Bert Lahr. They were all vaudeville stage actors before transitioning to movies. Frank Morgan, who played the bumbling Wizard and shifty Professor Marvel, started out acting in the silent films of the early 1900s. So these were all people who knew their craft well and had devoted their lives to it.

I was also struck by how young Judy Garland was. You just don't think about that kind of stuff when you're a kid. Anyone who's in a movie must necessarily be older and more important than you. But she was seventeen years old when she worked on *The Wizard of Oz.* Seventeen. She's so young that her voice is young and, for lack of a better word, pure. It's clear and unadulterated, which makes it all the more heartbreaking if you know anything about her life. I won't go into the details, but Metro Goldwyn Meyer movie studio used every bit of that poor woman's body and soul and then threw her out like trash when she couldn't make movies anymore. She self-destructed in a pit of despair, booze and pills. She died at the age of forty-seven.

As I watched it, I wondered for a moment why no one has tried to remake *The Wizard of Oz*—I hope no one does—and I think it might be one movie that's simply too iconic to touch. I can't even begin to fathom a cast that could compete, talent-wise, with the original. And I don't think even CGI could recreate the magic we all conjure in ourselves when we watch the original. There's nothing out there remotely like it. There's no other movie to even compare it to. It's an institution unto itself. (Writer, actor and director Kenya Barris has been talking about doing a re-imagining of the film since 2022. We'll see.)

Because I've watched this film my whole life and accepted it as much a part of life's mythos as Santa Claus, there were many specifics I never really considered as a kid. But when you think about it, *Oz* is an unusual movie because the protagonist is a little girl. Heck, we can hardly get little girl protagonists in movies these days, but *Oz* came out in 1939. Not only that, but she's a little girl hero who kills the villain. I mean, sure, it's all a dream, so technically she

doesn't kill the witch, but I don't think I really understood that as a kid. I thought that somehow, Dorothy's dream was real, and in fact, in the original *Oz* books by L. Frank Baum, *Oz* is a real place that Dorothy visits more than once.

The Wizard of Oz is so unusual, so rare, so weird, that these days, I proudly associate my state with the film. In fact, Kansas is a lot like the movie, in my opinion. Sure, we look boring and black-and-white from the outside, but there are a few fascinating gems to be found here, and even a fair amount of weirdness.

You just have to know where to look.

AMBER FRALEY is a native Kansan, journalist, essayist, storyteller, and wife and mom to the two greatest people in the world. She's the author of the darkly humorous essay collection From Kansas, Not Dorothy, and the viral essay Gen X Will Not Go Quietly, as well as numerous human-interest articles in regional magazines like KANSAS!. Growing up in Lawrence and Wichita, Amber spent her formative years with her face in a book or at the mall with her friends. She loves the Kansas with all her heart, is frequently awkward in public, and desperately wishes to see a tornado and live to tell the tale.

LANG JOHNNY MORE, BY BOBBIE LYN POWELL
ILLUSTRATION FROM "YOUNG ROBIN HOOD"

Mom Donna:

Jesse Scott & Keri Ault

***You Can't Get Rid of Me: An adopted son's search for family*, is the triumphant story of the survival and redemption of a gay kid adopted by evangelical parents who eventually finds not only his roots, but peace. This excerpt, from adoptee Jesse Scott's forthcoming memoir, is the first time Jesse and his brother Lee meet their biological mother. Available from Anamcara Press.**

We pull up in front of Donna's home and I hate to say it's the worst street in the neighborhood, but it's the worst street in the neighborhood. I take another deep breath. Part of me wants to run inside, yelling "I'm Here! I'm Here!" and another part of me feels like I need to smoke a whole pack of cigarettes. I'm relieved when Albert asks if I mind if we smoke one before going in. It hasn't occurred to me that he might be nervous too.

The door is opened by three kids, who are staring at us with big eyes. The oldest one turns around and yells, "They're here!"

The small hallway feels like it is filled with people immediately, but I realize it's just us and all these children. Albert introduces me to the kids, and they reach out their hand to shake mine. A young woman comes down the stairs. This is Jocelyn, their mother. Albert reminds me that Jocelyn is Pooken's daughter, and he lets me know that Jocelyn is legally deaf but can read some lips. I hold out my arms for a hug and she shyly gives me a squeeze.

The house is crammed with furniture, piles of laundry, and people. I look down the hall into the kitchen and see my mother sitting at the table. She's smoking a cigarette and she has her phone on the table. I make my way into the small room.

"Hi, Donna!"

"Oh, hi."

I'm immediately disappointed and floored by her indifference.

I ask if I can give her a hug.

"Well sure you can, son. It's nice to finally see you."

She doesn't get up, so I lean down and we awkwardly embrace. I have to be honest, it's not what I was expecting. She's definitely not beaming, and if anything she seems a little put off to the whole experience. Maybe she's overwhelmed. I'm definitely overwhelmed. The other people there are all talking at once and the kids are starting to bicker and I'm trying to have this moment I've waited for forever and part of me wants to yell at everyone to shut up and the other part wants to close my eyes and be back in Palm Springs. There is another part that just wants to crawl under the table with this woman and ask if this is finally really happening. I ask if I can sit, and she gestures toward the chair across from her.

I remember that I brought the jewelry to hand out, and ask if she would like to pick something out. She shrugs, looks at it for a minute, and tells me that I can pick something for her. I find a necklace with matching earrings that I think will compliment her style, which I'm not really clear about, but I say it anyway. I mean, she's 82 years old, but she definitely isn't dressed in the same conservative manner of my mother.

I try to make a big deal out of telling her it's the best quality of all the items I have to offer. She thanks me, but then shows me the necklace she is wearing. It contains a tiny amount of Duke's ashes. I can't compete with that, and then tell myself how dumb I am for thinking in those terms. I try not to react, as I spy the cockroaches scurrying around the kitchen floor. It reminds me of my days living in the SROs in downtown Portland. I guess I assumed she would be in a more comfortable place by now.

We talk for about an hour, and I tell her that Lee and Rosa are flying in tomorrow. I ask if she would like to stay in my hotel room with me, as there are two beds, and I feel like it might be easier than having to drive to this part of town before picking them up at the airport.

"Well, OK son. That might be nice. I can't remember the

last time I stayed in a hotel."

Jocelyn agrees to pack a bag for her, and Albert looks a little shocked that I'm making this suggestion. I'm kind of shocked at myself, but I feel like it might help us really spend some time together. Maybe my years of being a caregiver are showing, because when Jocelyn packs some Depends in her bag, I don't flinch.

I can definitely sense some tension between Albert and Donna in the car on the way to the hotel. I try to make small talk and ask about Jocelyn's kids, life in Philly in general, and the plans for the party that Albert is throwing us. He tells us that he's got the whole thing covered, and that we should just plan on showing up the day after tomorrow in the early afternoon. Honey tells us that she and her mom have been cooking for days, and I think I see Donna roll her eyes. OK. That makes a little more sense, I guess. She's got pride. After being in both Donna and Albert's houses, it makes sense why Albert is hosting the big get together, but I understand that might sting for her.

I'm trying to figure out what I should call her. "Donna" seems too casual, like we're pals or something. "Mom" doesn't feel right either. Not yet. In my head I'm calling her "Mom Donna" because my own mother is the person I call "Mom." So far I've gotten away with not calling her anything to her face. Maybe I should calm down and realize I'm only four hours into this thing, and that some of this stuff will work itself out.

We all have a cigarette outside the hotel room. I carry Donna's bag in, and she immediately chooses the bed closest to the bathroom. She looks around, and even though I warned her that it wasn't fancy, I think she's a little disappointed. We end up watching TV and ordering a pizza. That night I try to sleep, but between Donna's snoring and my racing mind, it's really difficult. There's a time difference too, so I give up on any plan on sleeping. I slip out of my room around 2 a.m. and call John. He's trying to be sweet and is acting like he's interested in hearing about all these new people. He lets me go on and on, and then quietly asks if I'm OK. I take a breath in between puffs on my cigarette.

"I'm OK. My head is swimming, but I'm glad I'm here. It's a lot. But I'm OK."

I can't decide if I will feel more relaxed with Lee and Rosa here, or if that will make it worse. I decide that it will be better, and that I can't worry about them. I go back to the room and somehow manage to drift off for a bit before Donna wakes me up to ask me where she can get a cup of coffee.

I admit that I was a little nervous about Lee's rough edges, but to be honest, Mom Donna seemed more comfortable around him. It was as if his rough edges helped put her to ease. Rosa is a social worker who inspects nursing homes, and is used to talking to older people she doesn't know. Even though I know she's still really depressed, she has rallied for this trip, and is even more chatty than I am, and so that helped us all start talking. We held up our glasses of beer and made a little toast, and at one point Rosa pulled out her phone to take a photo. Lee rolled his eyes and said, "Oh here we go!"

He and Donna looked at each other and said something obscene and then both of them looked right at the camera and flipped the bird, cackling together. They both have their long hair back in a ponytail, and besides Lee's goatee and knuckle tattoos, they look really similar. The expression on both of their faces is one of joy, and I'm so relieved that Lee didn't experience the same reception that I had from Donna. I'm telling myself that it's because I spent this time with her and she's more comfortable, but I think that anyone who looked at the two of them could instantly tell they are related. I don't say this out loud, but I wonder deep down if maybe Lee's dad is different from my own.

Lee and Rosa have a room in the same motel, and we decide to go back and hang out the rest of the day. We all have a cigarette outside before getting in the car and my mom's eyes light up when I hand over four packs of smokes that I bought for her at the bar.

My sister Christina and her husband Mike have driven down from New York, and they plan on coming by the hotel

to meet us. Christina is Albert's younger sister and is the person that I've had the most contact with on the phone besides Albert and my mom. Donna warns us that Christina's husband may try to talk to us about religion, and we all agree that he might have a hard sell in this crowd. We also agree to be polite. I'm so relieved when I meet Christina that she's enthusiastic about meeting us, immediately running up to me and Lee and giving us hugs.

"Hey Big Brothers! Oh my gosh, this is exciting!"

She talks a mile a minute, and she immediately starts teasing Donna about these handsome men she's been hiding from the rest of us. At one point she asks us where her husband Mike and Rosa are, and we realize they are in Lee's room. When I go knock on the door, Rosa gives me a look that says "Oh, thank God," as Mike has been preaching the gospel. I don't have a sense about him yet to know if it's something I can tease him about. Albert has been texting me all day about the party, and about how it's going, and he even stopped by briefly to meet Lee, who everyone is calling "Joe," which is short for José. He kept shaking his head and looking back and forth between Lee and Donna, just like everyone else.

Mom Donna has been telling us about how she met each of the men who are fathers to her kids. She met her first child's dad, Pedro, on Burnside street in Portland when she was a teenager. She tells us that she left Baby Pete with someone in the SRO while she was out working. She's very vague about it, but I think that's when he was removed from her care. Next thing she's talking about is being in Klamath Falls, Oregon, staying with Pedro's family. She tells me that Pedro, my dad, had a brother named Jesus, who I may be named after. She had Lee, "José," and somehow the two of us ended up at the Boys and Girls Aid Society. I try to remember what I learned from staying with Louann—stop paying attention to the dates and the details and listen to the stories. I also wonder again if Lee and I actually have the same dad. I pass for white most of the time, but of the two of us, I am the one who really looks like I have some Latin blood. Lee has always been blonde. I definitely don't bring this up. I wonder if, when we find Pete, he and I will look alike. I guess I won't be the oldest anymore.

We hear about how she met Bernard Hill, who was Pooken and Duke's dad. He was in the Air Force and was wearing a nice jacket. Donna told us they were in a bar where a fight broke out. Donna's shirt was ripped in the bustle of the chaos, and he gave her his jacket. The next time she saw him in that same bar, he came up to her and reminded her that she had his jacket. It doesn't seem like that smooth of a line to me, but apparently it worked, because she ended up staying with him for some time. She tells us she knew her family wouldn't let her come home with babies from a Black man, so she ended up following him north to Seattle, where she had Linda. They eventually made their way to Philly, but the couple separated when Donna was pregnant with Willina. Again, she doesn't tell us who ended up raising those kids.

Mom Donna met Albert Legg, who is Albert, Christina, and Gigi's dad. "He was OK, but he just kept going to jail," she says.

We all take turns going outside to smoke and we're shaking our heads at these crazy stories. Even though we don't say it out loud, there is an unspoken agreement to not push Donna into telling us why she gave us up, or why her other kids grew up in other homes besides hers. Instead, we focus on how proud she is of still being considered their mom, and as long as she has someone to pay attention to her stories, she is not shy. We also haven't asked her what she did to look for us, or about this fake photo of her missing kids.

That night, I realize that although it's still a little odd to be sharing a room with this woman I have just met, I am exhausted and fall off to sleep. I didn't realize how much tension my body had been holding, wondering how this was all going to go down. I think I was so busy worrying about the ways that it could be awful, that I'm starting to realize the ways this is actually pretty amazing. While it's not the instant connection I felt with Louann, and it's not the lifetime of mothering I had from my adopted mom, this is something different. I haven't quite settled into it yet, and neither has she, but it's feeling better. Definitely better than what it was like to be searching. I think.

JESSE SCOTT is a former case manager for people living with HIV, former caregiver, and is currently living out his retirement in the deserts of the West Coast. He continues to surprise people who have known him for years, for still being alive and kickin'.

KERI AULT is a social worker living in Portland, Oregon. Her writing has appeared in the Meadowlark Reader, *You Might Need to Hear This, Cirque, and Proof That I Exist.* When she is not writing or working, she is trying to spend as much time outside as possible, even when it's raining.

Idle Algorithms:

Peg Nichols

You receive via social media a message that appears to be a friend request, perhaps from a name you recognize. What an affirmative thought, someone wants you as a friend. An ideal concept, surrounding ourselves with a circle of friends.

A quick word of caution: stop to ask yourself: is this a genuine request from someone who knows you, or perhaps someone who has admired something you wrote in one of your posts and would like to know you better? On the other hand, is this from an algorithm that has just discovered that the two of you have in common a passion for kumquats and you both have ordered online size ten socks? Never mind that you ordered the socks as a present for your brother; the algorithm doesn't know what it doesn't know.

So you ponder. Will I hurt someone's sensibilities if I reject the request?

Reminds me of my brief career as a telephone operator. On rare occasions I would be removed from the local call board and assigned to one of the long-distance boards—you know, the tall instrument with a dozen cords, each with a plug on the unattached end. Back in those long-ago days when residential telephones were fixed to a wall.

In the early evening hours, supervision would be light and the lack of activity boring. I had a way to amuse myself that was never discovered and for which I was never fired. I could cause the telephones to ring in two houses at the same time. At each house someone would take the phone from the wall, thinking that the other party had called. As operators we were prohibited from monitoring the conversations, unless there was some reason to assure that the system was functioning properly; but listen in I did.

Often the dialogues were quite entertaining. "You called?" "No, you called." The most laugh-provoking were the calls

NEW RUN JUMP, KENT SMITH

that involved friends or people who recognized the other's voice. All the better if they were neighbors.

"My phone rang, so I answered. What are you calling me about."

"Do you have nothing more to do but ring the phone of someone you don't want to talk to?"

"You're right, I don't want to talk to you. We were having supper and we most certainly didn't want to be interrupted to leave the table and go answer the phone."

Slam.

It's odd, how returning the phone to the hook or cradle sounds different from a slam. You can just hear the difference.

One night I connected two of my dad's club friends who recognized each other's voices. One was immediately accusative. "If you're calling me to ask me to vote for you as club president, you're wasting your time."

"You're the one who called me, and if you think this is a way to solicit member's support, I hope you never run for state governor."

"I don't need your vote, vulgar, vulgar, vulgarity, but I'd give you mine ... for dog catcher."

Slam.

Slam.

My younger sister and Billy Long broke up. I connected those two lines and was excited when both my sister and Billy Long answered the phones.

"Billy?" my sister asked.

"Whaddya want?" Billy snarled.

"I was hoping you would call."

"I didn't call. You called me."

"You rang my phone," my sister insisted.

"Why would I want to talk to you?"

They continued to argue, but neither one could end the conversation until Billy's mother needed to use the phone. "I'll see you at school tomorrow," Billy concluded.

One of the conversations that always gave me the giggles when I thought about it was two of my mother's backyard neighbors, Mrs. Walker and Mrs. Thanton. They both said hello at the same time and recognized each other's voice.

After several long moments of silence, Mrs. Walker said, "You have me on the line, what did you want to talk about?"

"My phone rang. I picked it up," replied Mrs. Thanton.

"Likewise here. My phone rang. Why are you calling me?

"I did not call you."

"Then why did my phone ring?"

"I repeat. I did not call you. And since you have nothing to say I'm going to end this ridiculous conversation."

"Now that I have you on the line, I do have something to say," Mrs. Walker spat out. "I'd be grateful to you if you would keep your cat out of my garden."

"My cat does not—"

"Your cat certainly does. Comes to do its business in my garden. Digs up my vegetables, sometimes the marigolds, wherever it goes it scratches everything up. And I try to recover the damage, but sometimes the plants are so badly destroyed they can't be saved. You ought to keep that damned cat at home, don't let it wander around tearing up the neighborhood."

"I don't know what cat you are talking about, but it isn't my cat. You should pay closer attention before you start making accusations. There are other cats in this neighborhood, you know."

Slam.

"You think I can't trust my own eyes?"

Slam.

What made the conversation even funnier was the fact that apparently neither neighbor knew that often the offending cat was sleeping in front of my mother's gas-fired fireplace or eating from a special dish that my mother kept near the back door.

Hilarious as the conversations were, I always succeeded in keeping my laughter under control. Had I been discovered, I would have been out the door.

Long gone are telephone operators wielding long cords that link one caller with another. Connections are now made with mobile phones, transistors, integrated circuits, satellites, and even flux capacitors.

How nice to receive a friend request, but the recipient should be suspicious. Will the invitation to connect be the start of a meaningful relationship with a real, living, breathing individual, or is it an illusion? Does that person really want to be your friend, or has the suggestion come from an idle algorithm with too much time on its hands?

PEG NICHOLS landed in Kansas, by chance, stayed by choice. She is the author of ***Sidewalk Sale Across America***, a novel of the Harkins family survival through the Coronavirus epidemic.

THREE FACES, CATHY MARTIN

Fog:
Randy Kidd, D.V.M., PhD

I

Fog: Today is a foggy day. Very foggy. And I love it. Walking in the fog is refreshing—water droplets bathing and cooling skin, befogging glasses, matting down hair. I suppose it's the Irish in me; an ancient genetic code that relishes the reality and the mythology of mists, of fogs, of clouds.

Fog is, in reality, a cloud that has reached down to touch the ground. Thus, as we walk into the fog, we are metaphorically "walking on clouds." And those clouds we see in the sky are the ultimate "shape shifters"—giving our minds something new to imagine every step we take along the way.

Walking in the fog is, for me, a joy. Perhaps it's the mystery of what lies around the fog-hidden corner. Perhaps it is that you see more critters along the way—big eyes peering out from their hiding place behind the shroud of fog. At least it ***seems*** as if you see more critters.

Perhaps it's the quieting effect of the fog, as it wraps around all sense organs and blankets them from the hum and drum of civilization. Perhaps it's the memory of walking in the fogs of San Francisco when we lived there many years ago—thick nighttime fog rolling in from the sea, always to the accompaniment of throaty foghorns sounding their warnings across the Bay. The sound of many foghorns, muted in the clouds of fog, is hauntingly mesmerizing.

And so, there is a certain beauty surrounding fog. And fog's close cousin, ***mist***, has a similar, if slightly more muted, beauty and mystery about it.

II

Mist: Instead of fog, I could just as easily be walking in and enjoying mist—they are the same phenomenon, fog

just a denser variety of mist. So, you have almost exactly the same feeling, walking in mist or in fog, but when it comes to mystery and mystical tales, me thinks mist has a wee bit of an advantage over fog.

Perhaps it's just that ***mist*** has a more lyrical ring to it than does ***fog***. (Try saying them both out loud, and you'll hear what I mean.) And perhaps it's this resonance of sound-to-lyrics that the Irish poets so often rely upon to create a poem both melancholic and optimistic.

To be sure, both fog and mist have the same literal meaning: water in the form of droplets floating or falling in the atmosphere at or near the surface of the earth and approaching the form of rain. For those of scientific mind, mist is less-thick fog. ***Fog*** is the name given to resulting visibility less than one kilometer (1,093.6 yards or 0.621371 miles); on a ***misty*** morn, you can still see things at least 1000 meters (one kilometer) down the trail.

III

Haze, Smoke, and Smog are additional terms that, when spoken aloud, sound much harsher than fog, or mist, or cloud. It could be that they sound harsher … because they are harsher.

Haze is composed of small dry particles in the air that, by themselves, are invisible … until together they become a dense enough congregation to make the sky appear as if it is shrouded in a thin veil of milky gauze, glittering in the sunlight. ***Smoke*** is, of course, created when something is burned … and the ashes from the burning reach into the skies. ***Smog*** is a term created in the early 1900's to describe the combination of smoke and fog—a sooty combination that had, by then, become a common phenomenon around areas populated heavily by humans.

And so be it for the realities behind the additives to our skies; for me the real interest lies in the stories – the symbology, mythologies and mysteries—we have built around them.

IV

Watery Skies: I suppose we should expect any alteration to our skies to carry within it some mysterious symbology along with its resultant mythological story. Humans have always looked to the skies for spiritual guidance, and a guide that can seemingly shape-shift at will is certainly worthy of being the creator of stories.

Childhood is a time to lie on your back, look up into the clouds, and make up your own stories as to what wild creatures you are seeing and what they are doing. Or at least it should be your time for that. The stories you can tell your young mind are constantly changing as the clouds move across the horizon, as they shift from one shape to another.

Here in Kansas even the adults watch the clouds as they are constantly shifting—hoping that the next winds don't bring in the rotating wall cloud buried in ominous green skies—skies punctuated by lightning bolts thrown by Zeus or, in another story, that have come from the beak of the Thunderbird. Kansans know that this kind of sky can quickly turn into the full-blown tornado that transports Dorothy and Toto into another world.

It's no surprise, then, that clouds have many metaphorical meanings—for novelists, playwrights, and songwriters (and memoirists). For these, as well as for poets and philosophers, watery skies (clouds and fog and mist) may be the most useful metaphors of all time.

You can make a cloud or mist or fog be a character in your story. Or any of them can stand for bad things (a love affair gone bad, for one example, or as a philosophy with bad consequences). Or they can represent something hidden … or something that needs to hide. And they can be used to stand in for any of the many incarnations of a soul.

Or in modern times, the cloud may be where reams of data are stored—a storage that involves huge human-built warehouse areas and massive computer servers that are powered and cooled by mechanically-induced energetics.

V

Last Words: And so, me thinks that clouds and mists and fog offer metaphors too vast to wrap our heads around, too elusive to ever catch up to, too squiggly to ensnare in any web we might cast, were we ever able to run them down.

I turn to Joni Mitchel's "Both Sides Now" to help me understand clouds and fog and mist a bit better. To recognize that maybe the best we can do is to realize that it is, after all, life's illusions we really recall. Reality is, and will always be, shrouded within the clouds and fogs and mists Nature creates for us.

"I really don't know life at all." Line from"Both Sides Now" —by Joni Mitchel.

RANDY KIDD, D.V.M., Ph.D. holds doctorates in Veterinary Medicine from The Ohio State University and Veterinary and Clinical Pathology from Kansas State University. After practicing traditional veterinary medicine for many years, he opened Honoring the Animals, a holistic practice in Kansas City, Missouri. Dr. Kidd was the author of two books including "Dr Kidd's Guide to Herbal Care For Dogs," a columnist for multiple pet care magazines including Dogs Naturally and Herbs for Health. He was Past President of the American Holistic Veterinary Medical Association and a leader in many other civic and nature-oriented organizations. Retired from active practice, he continued writing, speaking and teaching on the big topic of "Reuniting The Human Spirit With The Soul Of Nature." And just like a rabbit playing tricks, he died on January 15, 2024, toward the end of the Year of the Rabbit!

The Truth Never Rhymes:
Chuck Warner

When I was sixteen, I attended Southeast High School in Wichita, Kansas. My closest guy friends were all bright and usually took those academically challenging honor classes. Me, not so much. Although I expected to attend college, my test scores paled compared to theirs.

The thing I enjoy about being around smart people is that they frequently possess a wicked sense of humor. Such was the case with those four friends of mine.

The five of us were hanging out one day after school. Apparently, three of my friends in A.P. English had been studying anti-proverbs; those altered and humorous versions of standard proverbs. For example, "One should try everything once except incest and folk dancing," or "if you aren't the lead dog, the scenery never changes." It seemed they couldn't get enough of them and wanted to keep the vibe going. As a result, we began making up anti-proverbs in one of our cars in the school parking lot. Like high school boys who think they are budding stand-up comics, we chuckled at our own cleverness as we transformed well-known proverbs to make them funny.

For some reason I remember my lame contribution was "the truth never rhymes."

Although my homemade adage was pure gibberish, at least it reminded me of Mark Twain's rather perplexing saying, "History doesn't repeat itself, but it often rhymes." Also, I thought it sounded kind of pithy. Like an old proverb, it was a bit inscrutable with a skosh of pretentiousness.

Regardless of whether the truth rhymed or not, when I was in high school, I gave very little thought to the concept of truth. I mostly assumed it matched the definition found in most dictionaries; something like truth is the body of real things, events, and facts known with great certainty. However, as I have grown older, the truth seems more fluid and less certain, not so black and white.

Even our judicial system shows signs of how the truth is sometimes squishy. Although courts are adamant about finding the truth, it doesn't always happen. Witnesses promise to tell the truth, "Nothing but the truth," but sometimes they lie or are mistaken about something they saw or heard. For instance, the development of scientific DNA testing in the 1980s resulted in hundreds of convictions subsequently being overturned and prisoners exonerated. In other words, what was considered the truth years earlier is now proved to be inaccurate.

Speaking of science, even though scientists go to great lengths to verify their findings, not all their colleagues agree. For example, even if we seemed to have settled the flat earth issue, we are still arguing climate change and the once settled fluoridated water debate.

Obviously, those disputes remind me of the current political discourse where the simple telling of the truth takes on the appearance of a dumpster-fire. Also, it is no coincidence that all scientific papers are presented in the form of an "argument," because other scientists might not accept the truth of their scientific evidence.

Another obstacle to the search for absolute truth is how the English language evolves over time. To illustrate, in 2022 the Merriam-Webster Dictionary defined racism as "a belief that race is the primary determinant of human traits and capacities and that racial differences produce an inherent superiority of a particular race."

According to CNN on June 12, 2022, Kennedy Mitchum, a recent law school graduate, called the dictionary to task suggesting their definition limited racism to only those who dislike someone merely because of the color of their skin. As a result, if you were not a member of the Ku Klux Klan and other white supremacy groups, you might not consider yourself a racist. Mitchem claimed that racism was more nuanced and should include systemic conditions and microaggressions, that include those who fail to call out the more subtle discrimination.

According to the article, after further review the dictionary agreed to broaden the definition as she suggested, as evidence of how truth is subject to change. What was maybe the truth fifty years ago, changed after such events as the Ferguson Missouri race riots and George Floyd.

Another example of how truth can be elusive is the area of history. Readers usually accept events in history books as truthful because they have been thoroughly researched from multiple reliable sources and are meticulously fact-checked prior to publication. Even so, I am reminded how history is traditionally told by the victors who bring their own biases to the table.

As Chinua Achebe, a prominent Nigerian novelist and essayist said in a 1994 interview in the *Paris Review*, "There is that great (African) proverb—that until the lions have their own historians, the history of the hunt will always glorify the hunter."

Although family stories and memoirs are a form of history, most readers assume events from memoirs are accurate, not because of documented research, but because the writer witnessed the events firsthand. However, according to author and memoirist Mary Karr, "Memoir is not an act of history but an act of memory, which is innately corrupt."

As a result, both histories and memoirs are flawed by the writer's memory and biases. Add to that, now that I am in my seventies and many of those events in my life occurred a long time ago, well, my memory isn't what it used to be.

Incidentally, despite acknowledging my own memory might be compromised, my first attempts at memoir writing caused me to avoid input from other family members. I made that decision out of some misguided pride that the stories should be mine alone even if the accuracy of a certain event might be flawed, or forgotten, or another family member might remember incidents differently. However, I recently concluded the more the merrier and began asking family members to unpack their memories about our family stories. Even if all our collective memories are equally imperfect, the most important benefit of family input is that they sustain the common family bonds. And it is the act of sharing those memories, regardless of whether the stories recall a poignant moment or provoke a belly laugh, they bring families together. Such an activity is important, especially if individually we have different beliefs and outlooks on life.

Family stories can connect and unite relatives, rather than divide. They help focus on the importance of family by emphasizing what we have in common rather than on where we might disagree.

In the end, I suppose it's not important whether the truth rhymes or not. What matters is we recognize the even the truth sometimes gets skewed by bias and perception. As a result, when confronted with purported truth, consider the source or the circumstances before accepting it, much less passing it on. Also, we should not settle for the truth being merely close to factual because "close only counts in horseshoes and hand grenades."

CHUCK WARNER grew up in Wichita and has lived in Lawrence since the 1960s, when he first attended KU. With business and law degrees he enjoyed a nearly forty-year career in business and banking. After retiring in 2007, he began writing about his maternal grandfather, which resulted in the University Press of Kansas publishing ***Birds, Bones, and Beetles: The Improbable Career and Remarkable Legacy of University of Kansas Naturalist Charles D. Bunker*** in 2019. In 2020 his book was recognized as a Kansas Notable Book, awarded both the best Kansas history and book layout by the Kansas Authors Club, and a High Plains Book Awards finalist. His essays have been published in ***The Write Bridge, 105 Meadowlark Reader,*** and ***Write from the Center.***

Ellen's Idol:

Beth Gulley

The first trigger was her use of the word "idol." "Elvis was my idol" were her exact words. Anyone who ever read the Exodus story about the golden calf knows perils of idol worship. Those poor Israelites either fell into a sink hole or had to drink powdered golden calf in shame.

The second trigger was that she saw Elvis at the movies. According to the Nazarene Manual, Nazarenes did not go to the movie theater. They did not support the evils of Hollywood. The year before, I went to see a 007 movie with friends from school and then spent months riddled with guilt from lying to my parents.

This woman, who looked like she'd never had a day of fun in her whole life, just confessed flippantly that she had been to the movies loads of time and that Elvis Presley had been her idol. My doors of perception cracked open in a rude awakening.

Up to this moment, I thought this woman lived for shuttling her kids to and from school, making food for other people to enjoy, and going to church. Now I envisioned her as a teenager at the movie theater swooning over a young Elvis Presley, imagining she was the actress playing his sweetheart de jour.

Who knew middle aged ladies with bad haircuts and powerful, conservative husbands could have backstories and dreams incongruent with their present? Lesson learned.

BETH GULLEY lives and works in the Kansas City area. She teaches English at Johnson County Community College. She has nine books of poetry including *Frog Joy*, runner up for the Amity Prize in 2023, and *Since Corona Ruined Our Trip to the Library,* winner of the Kansas Authors Club Chapbook Prize in 2023. Recently, she published in *105 Meadowlark Reader, What's the Deal With Alien Buddha Part 2,* and *365 Days: A Poetry Anthology.* She is part of the Kansas Author's Club, the Riverfront Reading group and the Writers Place.

No Peace, No Peace In Greece!:

Louis Copt

I heard a story recently about a woman who remembers everything—each moment etched into her mind like carvings in stone, from childhood weather patterns to the color of her socks on an ordinary Tuesday. I envy her. Most days, I can't recall last night's dinner. But there are moments, scattered through time, that refuse to stay buried. They linger—surfacing in the stillness of a shower, beneath the drone of a lawn mower, or with the crunch of toast beneath my teeth. Why do some memories claw their way back while others remain hidden behind a veil of fog, elusive and undefined like fruit cocktail suspended in lime Jell-O?

Behind that fog, a sharp scene emerges: Northern Greece. A cold gray morning grips a desolate town. My wife and I, strangers to the land, carry everything we own in a battered Boy Scout backpack and a few plastic bags. Days-old raisins from Athens are our only sustenance. Ahead, the border to Yugoslavia beckons like a shadowy promise, unknown and unavoidable. No bus, just empty miles stretched between us and the next town.

Hitchhiking blurs memory, each ride blurring into the next—a truck, a silent stranger, a ride forgotten the moment it ends. But this border crossing carves itself into permanence. A vast plain framed by mountains and barbed wire. Cold wind howls across the emptiness. Out of the fog emerges a lone man in a military box. His laughter slices through the wind.

"Why you go?" he sneers. "No bus. Yugoslavia that way. Walk."

And so we walk. Each step forward feels surreal. I think, Who has walked this road before? Why am I here, marching into the unknown? But there is no turning back. Adventure—or perhaps madness—awaits ahead.

Closer now, the distant figures of soldiers come into view, drab uniforms blending into the bleakness, German shepherds straining at their leashes. Machine guns glint under the pale sky.

My heart quickens as we approach. The red star on the soldier's hat looms larger than life. For a fleeting, absurd moment, I want his hat.

"Look, hippies!" he barks, gesturing to his comrade. "Americans?"

"Yes," I answer, my voice steady despite the chill crawling up my spine. He snatches our bags and demands our passports before disappearing into his box. The door shuts behind him with a metallic clang that reverberates through the empty landscape. We are left standing there, exposed and powerless, our fate sealed behind that closed door. I imagine every nightmare scenario—false accusations, planted drugs, a one-way ticket to some forgotten gulag. The wind howls.

Time stretches endlessly.

Finally, the door creaks open. He emerges with our belongings, unreadable eyes scanning us. "Where you go?"

"Skopje," I say. "Is there a bus?"

His laughter is a bitter echo across the plain. "No bus," he grins. "You walk. Forty kilometers."

We nod, shoulders heavy under the weight of our burden, and begin walking. The barren landscape stretches endlessly, broken only by wind-swept fields. I imagine sleeping in a barn, wondering if we'll find shelter before night falls. But then, a miracle—dust rises in the distance.

A bus rattles toward us.

We wave frantically, hope igniting as it roars closer. The bus, packed with peasant workers, barrels past. For a moment, despair sets in. But then—brake lights. The bus halts. Through a storm of negotiation, the door creaks open. We climb aboard, squeezed into a mass of humanity —black shawls, gold teeth, laughter, and jostling hands making space where none exists.

"They must think we're from the moon," I whisper to Phyllis. She smiles despite the chaos.

Thirty minutes later, the bus shudders to a stop in Skopje. As we disembark, warm smiles and waves follow us. I offer the driver money, but he shakes his head. Instead, I press a Kennedy half-dollar into his hand. “Souvenir from the USA,” I say.

Evening settles over Skopje, and another adventure begins. As I hoist the Boy Scout backpack, my gaze lingers on the blackened mark where a peace sign once was—erased by an angry Greek customs officer who had shouted as he crossed it out with a thick marker:

“No peace! No peace in Greece!”

The irony settles in, as sharp and strange as a spoonful of lime Jell-O. Some moments are unforgettable, even without a single bite of toast to summon them back.

LOUIS COPT has been painting professionally since 1976. He received a BA in art from Emporia State University in 1971, and also studied at the Art Students League of New York. He recently was the focus of a feature article in American Artist, which is based in New York and is one of the oldest art publications in the country. Collectors of Louis’ work include the Kansas City Chiefs, H&R Block, Texas A&M, Federal Home Loan Bank, the University of Kansas, Kansas State University, the Overland Park Convention Center, CrossFirst Bank, and private collectors across the country. In 2011 he was named Governor’s Artist by the Kansas Arts Commission.

Feathery Accomplices:

Hope Lake, PhD

The Sunflower Jungle" as I call it, grew up not by any hard work I did, but by the aid of my feathery accomplices. Yes, the mourning doves with their salmon-colored legs and intricately patterned blue-and-white under-wing feathers, as glamorous as peacock tails, helped create it.

The pair of cardinals that come by mid-morning or early evening and never stay long, are a delight to watch. It's supposed to be good luck to see a cardinal in your garden. I'm blessed with the returning pair. They peck at the black oil sunflower seeds for a few minutes, but fly off at the hint of any other creature coming to the feast.

The red-throated "purple" finches usually eat from the hanging feeder, unlike the wide variety of sparrows that feed on the ground. Occasionally, a goldfinch graces my garden with its bright yellow and gold colors. I wish I could hear their songs, but when I'm outside, the road noise drowns them out, and when I'm inside, my many thick-paned windows that keep the cold and heat out, also stop those lovely tones.

When the bluejay shows up, the other birds tend to flee, but he never stays long. The spring-loaded feeder keeps him from those seeds. He doesn't seem to like to feed from the ground that much.

Earlier this spring, my yard was filled with grackles, not my favorite bird, though they have gorgeous iridescent coloring. Grackles are greedy, chasing other birds away. But this year, there were red-winged blackbirds in the flock, and they are delightful to watch. When I was preteen there was a song about "little red-wing." I believe she was a Native American, but I always connect the happy times connected to that song with red-winged blackbirds.

I'm forgetting my other accomplices, the half dozen or so squirrels that devour the seeds, too. I put plenty of seed out so there is enough for all. .I enjoy watching them sit up and look around before stooping to grab seeds in their prehensile paws. They remind me of the prairie dogs that I loved to watch in Hutchinson when I lived there. My favorites are the two red squirrels. The first I named Robbie, though I don't know if it is a male or female. He/she is a watchful but slow eater. The smaller red is a fast eater, bobbing up and down to grab up seed and chomp on it or fill his/her cheeks and be sure he/she is safe.

These accomplices left many, many seeds uneaten, resulting in the six-foot tall sunflowers that overwhelmed the rest of the plants last summer and are threatening to do the same this spring.

I tried pulling some of the plants up and leaving some strategically placed so that they would complement the various types of lavender and irises. But the spring rains have beaten me. The jungle is growing again.

Sunflowers are my adult son's favorite flower, so I'm not trying too hard to keep them under control. Besides, my "feathery accomplices" feed on their seeds long after the blooms have dried out.

HOPE LAKE PHD, writes short fiction, poetry, plays and children's picture books. Lake's awards include the 2024 Walter Williams Award in Missouri and Coffin Memorial Book Award in Kansas for *OUR MOTHERS' GHOSTS and Other Stories.* An active member of the KAC, she lived in Hutchinson for 16 years. Currently, she resides near her family in Columbia, Missouri, with her canine companion, Hugo.

Not An Accomplice:
Hope Lake, PhD

When we were eight or nine, I helped my best friend Sara June deceive her blind grandmother by helping her hide her raincoat, boots, rain hat and umbrella under the front porch because Nanny, as we called her, insisted that Sara wear them anytime rain was predicted, even if there was only a ten per cent chance.

What a rush we felt as Sara shed the raingear! We quickly shoved it out of sight and ran to Horace Mann's schoolyard to play. Tired and satisfied, we would return to Sara's front yard, retrieve her raingear, dress Sara in it again, and say goodbye. Yes, we were deceitful eight and nine year old accomplices, but also just two young girls who wanted to play.

I was complicit in teenage crimes also. In Illinois, girls could buy and drink alcohol at the age of 18. Boys had to be 21. I bought many a six-pack or bottle of wine for parties, or for boys I liked, during the three years before it was legal for them to drink.

But there came a time when I regretted my refusal to be an accomplice. When my mother asked me to help her end her life.

My mother had a rare form of diabetes known as brittle. It required constant monitoring with urine tests throughout the day and having insulin injections as needed, often several times a day. As her condition got worse, she not only used regular insulin but also NPH insulin that was stronger, and more expensive.

Doctors advised her to smoke to stave off hunger pangs, and she became a chain smoker all her remaining days. Ten years into her diagnosis, the doctors at Deaconess Hospital in Boston sent her home with the prognosis that she might possibly live another nine years. At that time I was in fourth grade, and my family had just adopted my younger brother who was six. My older brother had graduated from high school and joined the army.

Mother had a survivor's spirit and wanted to live until all three of her children were grown and out on their own. She learned everything she could about the disease, and survived much longer than the doctors predicted.

The diabetes took a huge toll on her body. It wasted away. The fat was eaten up by the constant insulin shots that kept her alive, her arteries hardened by diabetes and smoking. She had her first of several strokes when I was sixteen. Fortunately, it happened after school was out for the summer, and I was able to care for her.

The family bought me a car so that I could drive her to doctor's appointments, get groceries and help her recover. By fall she had recovered her ability to talk and use her right side again. I continued to drive her and my younger brother wherever they needed to go when my father was working, or not available.

Because of hardening of the arteries, her right leg was amputated from just below the knee. Still, she attended my younger brother's high school graduation in a wheel chair with her stump covered by a skirt. She taught herself to get in and out of bed to use the commode, and she could get in and out of her wheelchair to get around the house. It was a difficult and painful life for her.

By 1964, I was married and moved away from my hometown across the state, but I wrote her everyday, and insisted on trips to see my mother and family as much as possible. On one such trip, when we were alone in her room, my mother asked me to help her take a bottle full of sleeping pills that she had accumulated over a matter of months.

"Please, honey! I'm ready to go," she pleaded. "Your dad is looking at nursing homes for me in St. Louis. I want to die here with my garden that I can see from the window and my friends that call on me from time to time."

"Mom, don't ask me to do this. I love you too much to lose you."

"If you love me, please help me."

"I can't, Mom. I don't want you to die."

"But, I don't want to live anymore. I pray at night that I will die in my sleep."

"God must want you to live longer."

"To suffer more?"

"No, to be a role model. To help others understand diabetes. You've taught so many about living with this disease. Please, Mom, don't do this. I'm so sorry. I just can't help you."

Silence. Then she motioned me to the bed. She reached out her arms for me to come and hug her. We hugged and kissed each other's cheeks. She told me she understood. Asked me not to worry.

She did go to a nursing home within a few weeks. It was in St. Louis because the Alton nursing homes didn't have staff trained to take care of someone with her level of diabetes. I visited her there only a couple of times before she died. To my relief the subject never came up again.

I didn't have the courage to be her accomplice then. I wonder if I would now.

Now that I remember the two additional years she lived in and out of hospitals, in a nursing home away from friends and family, until she had her third stroke and fourth and final heart attack at the age of 52.

I was 24. Do I wish I had helped her two years earlier? Yes, I do.

Would I have the courage now? I don't know. I'll never know.

HOPE LAKE PHD, writes short fiction, poetry, plays and children's picture books. Lake's awards include the 2024 Walter Williams Award in Missouri and Coffin Memorial Book Award in Kansas for *OUR MOTHERS' GHOSTS and Other Stories.* An active member of the KAC, she lived in Hutchinson for 16 years. Currently, she resides near her family in Columbia, Missouri, with her canine companion, Hugo.

My Failed Religious Training:
Dan Nagengast

I'm told I was baptized as an infant in the Dalton Presbyterian Church. I just can't remember it. Once diaper trained, I began attending Sunday School in the church annex, a cinder block building built by the farmers in the church. I do recall being an angel in the Christmas pageant. We were trotted out with little wire halos, and coached through a halting, and wildly distracted version of Away In The Manger, which stole the show.

This was followed, relentless Sunday School after relentless Sunday School, with bible story education, plus a week of Bible School in the summer. I have a cloisonné attendance pin, with little cloisonné attendance ribbons attached by chains, which hang down two to three inches. I really don't have occasion to wear it on my chest much, but it is kind of like a military decoration.

So, through all that, I learned many bible stories, though, I've never read the Bible, and only now have I come to understand that my Sunday School teachers were hiding all the good stuff.

As soon as I left home, my church-going days were finished for almost 15 years, aside from an occasional Christmas Eve or invite to Passover.

My father was raised a Catholic, and had gone to a rural Catholic School as a child, but his distaste for the nuns who taught him, lead him to leave that church forever. My mother was raised as a Southern Baptist in Arkansas, but she also never latched on, so I guess my lack of fervor is multi-generational. I would never criticize anyone for their faith; that is, unless it leads them to do evil in the world. The occasions to do that have, indeed, arisen.

When I arrived in the more Islamic regions of West Africa, I found that I could readily share biblical stories with Muslims. And they knew who Jesus was, and admired him.

Many Arabic/ Islamic names are cognates of Bible names: Abraham/Ibrahim, Adam and Eve/Adama and Awa.

Around smoldering fires at night, we could tell each other Old Testament stories.

When I went to work for Church World Service in Senegal, I was asked if I wanted to become a missionary for the Presbyterian Church during my service. I had met several missionaries, primarily from the U.S. and Ireland, during my time, and I will write about that at some point.

Medical missionaries were doing good work. I found many evangelical missionaries to be disruptive and dismissive of the cultures they were working in, though I am sure not all are like that.

In Islamic countries, I was always invited to mosque, and to pray with people, when asking for rain, etc. I politely did so, and would mimic the prayers, as, honestly, I would do in American churches. I just was trying to show respect for people's religious beliefs. And I do not deny those beliefs, which I deem personal to them. I also realize that churches and mosques are social glue of a type, that often guards against disruptive behavior, and tries to raise up the generations coming along with rules that safeguard against violence, greed or destructive sexual impulses. In many ways, religious institutions serves as nurturing communities in which to raise and protect children.

On the other hand, I don't think it can be denied that, like all human institutions, they often can be used and exploited by self-centered and narcissistic individuals with a will to power, to feed destructive appetites, or a twisted desire to inflict punishment on others as a mean to consolidate power. Religion has always been fertile ground for scandal and a figure like Martin Luther was rare, as he tried to punch up, when all too often religious movements and devotion are exploited to punch down on the less powerful. I find an inability to see that is a pretty willful inability.

I found Church World Service and its activities to be generally compatible with my world view, and the staff strove to be in the world, the gentle, unifying force that they imagined Jesus to have been. At any rate, converting Muslims or Animists was never expected of me.

When I returned to the U.S., I continued to work for CWS, organizing hunger walks, and lining up grain gifts from farmers for overseas famine relief. I traveled around the state, working with almost all the denominations in their shared concerns for the hungry. It is not necessarily an equally-shared concern, but it exists, and in the non-Christian religious communities as well.

It made me realize that a lot of people are in church pews or at the mosque, who are there for the community, and some of the doctrine is the thing that needs to be professed in order to remain in good standing. That peculiar human proclivity is not confined to religion. I find that people who want to be a part of a political party often have to profess things that absolutely contradict their observations, inclinations and life experiences. I once gave a slide show about Sub-Saharan Africa to a group of Holdeman Mennonites. Just excellent people, who, though they dressed plain, and eschewed much of higher education, also drove the biggest John Deeres and had nice Hondas. As part of the slide show, I noted mid-Sahara petroglyphs that indicated the desert was substantially wetter about 18,000 years ago. I thought nothing of it, but a friend who I had been working with came up to me after, and said, "You know, we only believe the world is about 4,000 to 6,000 years old. How long ago did you say that rock art was made?" I cringed, and said, 'Scientists think about 18,000 years go." He grinned and said, "Oh, I guess we can live with that." Dogma was agreed to, but not necessarily believed.

After Lynn and I married, and when our first child came along, we joined a Mennonite church in Topeka. This was in a time of strife in the Near East, of all places, and a goodly part of our reckoning was that by joining a "peace" church, we could offer our children an easier get-out-of- war-free card, should the draft be reinstituted.

Plus, I thought the kids should learn bible stories so that they would have something to talk about with Muslim kids one day. We had not realized that we were joining a group of warm, caring families who would help raise our children as caring adults. We had not realized that a group of those families would become our closest friends, with whom we would share life's joys and perils and milestones. We had not realized that these Mennonite families would not overly concern themselves with what we believed, or where we would be spending eternity.

And so we joined that community, or at least were hangers-on, while never professing our faith. While the members of the church had been so for many generations, we newcomers were always welcome. And I don't think we alone in the pews, were the only non-believers.

Our kids grew up. We moved away. Our Sunday mornings are mellow and slow now. We maintain our church friendships. I have known people of several faiths, many of whom I would trust to raise my children as well as I did. Some, I feel could have done a better job. I believe that when I die, I will be accepted back into the same earth from which I arose. The earth will have a good and productive use for me, without subjecting me to an eternity of lyre music or hellfire.

DAN NAGENGAST grew up on a farm in the Nebraska Panhandle. After small town things he eventually ended up in law school in NYC. He followed that with 8 years in villages in West Africa. He has lived in Kansas since 1984, serving as director for Church World Service, Executive Director for the Kansas Rural Center, and owner of Seeds From Italy, farming throughout with his wife Lynn Byczynski.

New York:
Kathy Roberts

In February of 2003, I boarded a train in Lawrence, Kansas headed for New York City. I had never taken a train before but flying was out of the question. Actually, everything had become impossible. Grocery shopping, staying sober until noon, watching TV, leaving the house, all had become too difficult for me. Fear of bank repossession was the only thing getting me on a train for New York. It was, I suppose, an act of survival. I was a toy representative and, if I wanted to keep the house I was spending so much time not leaving, I would need to attend Toy Fair. I also had a job interview. It was too overwhelming to think too far ahead.

The train was scheduled to leave Lawrence around 5:30 am. It was to arrive in New York City around noon the following day. My job interview was scheduled for 8 p.m. It was a dinner thing which would allow me time to check into my hotel, freshen up and get to the designated restaurant where I was to meet the woman who might save my house. I didn't really think I was cutting it close. I even thought I would be able to get in a nap before meeting up with her. I was optimistic. Very optimistic since I had been unable to sleep more than a couple of hours per night since my partner Sue's death five months prior. Actually, optimism might be overstating my mindset. I was pretty sure nothing in the world could phase me anymore, sleepwalking through the rest of my life seemed fine but I didn't want to end up living out my remaining days under a bridge.

The first sign of trouble came very early on. The train was several hours late picking me up. I needed to make a connection in Chicago but there was a seriously long layover there so I thought I was still OK. It seems that Amtrak creates a schedule in much the same way a blind man plays darts. Since my only previous experience had been with airlines, I thought that they were actually using the schedule as a kind of plan that would enable it's passengers to make commitments. Instead it is an inside joke used to baffle foreign travelers used to a viable rail I and novice Americans.

Truthfully, a late train wasn't my main problem. My main problem was that I was crazy. I hadn't read Joan Didion's "Year of Magical Thinking," yet, so I didn't have confirmation of that fact. But deep down I knew it was true. Watching my partner die unexpectedly had derailed me. Since her death, I avoided any situation that did not afford a clear and immediate exit.

Therefore, I could go to the grocery store, meander down the aisles picking out food choices but I could not manage to stand in line to pay. The moment someone got in line behind me, I would pretend I had forgotten something, excuse myself and start the arduous task of returning all the products in my cart to their proper place on the shelf. I was a reverse shopper. I was an unpaid shelf stocker. Sensing that this behavior was not falling within the normal range, I tried shopping at several different grocery stores. It was the same plan I used to purchase alcohol. I was going to 10 different liquor stores to avoid anyone thinking I might have a drinking problem. I didn't want to establish a noticeable pattern. I did, however, want to drink.

The train was preferable to the airplane because, as everyone knows, there is no way off a plane once it is in the air. I had seen enough old movies to know that all trains come equipped with a cord, that when pulled, brings the train to an immediate stop. I hoped I wouldn't have to use it but I felt better knowing it was an option.

I had a couple of books, some music and my laptop to amuse me during the overnight trip. I took my seat and immediately felt like no one wanted to sit with me. I didn't want anyone to sit with me but I also didn't want people to avoid sitting with me. I reasoned that people were passing the open seat because I am fat. They didn't want to sit next to a giant, fat woman.

Also, I was crying. But I figured it was the fat thing. Actually, I couldn't seem to quit crying. It was chronic, like hay fever.

I wasn't sobbing or anything. There was just a constant, pathological dripping from my eyes and my nose. Also, I never had any tissues. For someone with pathological crying disorder, this was a major oversight. I sniffed constantly until that wouldn't resolve the problem. Then I would search everywhere for something to help the situation. The result was blowing my nose on napkins, newspapers and magazine pages. Also, I carried a pint of bourbon everywhere I went. A friend had told me that it wasn't physically possible to feel anxiety while you are drinking. Eureka! I overlooked the part where she ended up escorted out of work to a waiting car which took her to rehab. A solution is a solution even if it creates more problems than it solves. Look at gas engines and how long it took for that to become a major deal.

We were several hours late getting into Chicago but I was still able to make my connection. Chicago to New York was a far more crowded train and empty seats were few and far between. I took a seat at the end of a car, near the door. People tended to avoid these seats in the winter because it is very drafty, far away from the restrooms and people are always stepping out for a cigarette. I reasoned I would be left pretty much alone and I was impervious to discomfort. That is one of the perks of insanity. You can suffer a lot of things that would ordinarily be problematic, like frostbite.

But, as stated, the train was filling up and eventually I had a seatmate. He was a linebacker sized man with a look that said, "Leave me the Hell alone!" I was happy to oblige. In front of me, another giant, glowering man sat down. I wasn't really afraid of anything anymore except spiders, airplanes, lines at the grocery store, conversations, people telling me I was going to be okay and the thought of going through a day unmedicated. Large, sullen men took a backseat to my nervous breakdown. The only thing that bothered me was it made me aware of the fact that I was crying. I felt, on a social level, I should try to stop or hide my tears. Since the first wasn't possible, the second option was my only choice. I stared out the window, trying to mask my sharp breath intake with sighs. I'm not sure why I thought loud sighing was

preferable to crying. As usual, I did not have any tissues which meant I would have to crawl over the giant man and find my way to the restroom. I stood up and made my way to the aisle. My seatmate said, "Don't leave your bag. This is a train and stuff gets stolen!" The man in the seat in front of us offered, "Yeah, don't leave anything you want to see again." I can't say for sure why this caused me to completely fall to pieces, but it did. And I don't cry pretty. My face squishes up and turns red and my nose runs like a faucet. I managed, "I'm sorry," grabbed my bag and hurried to the closest restroom. I am certain that I freaked them out and I didn't want to have to go back and face them. So, I stayed in the bathroom until people started knocking. I remembered why I was on the train to begin with. I tried to recreate the train car in my head, searching for the miracle cord that could stop the train and let me off. I couldn't find it using my mind's eye so I sheepishly left the bathroom and began scouring the train for the life-saving cord. I don't think I would have pulled it but I sure wanted to know there was some way out of this trip if I just couldn't stand it.

I got back to my seat and the giant men were deep in conversation. They stopped talking as I approached. My seatmate said, "Little sister, we've been talking and you seem very sad. It's a long trip. Do you want to talk?"

The other man kneeled on his seat, hugging the head rest and regarded me with compassionate interest. I could tell you how nice it was for them to care about a perfect stranger and that they now looked like angels to me instead of imposing men. I could tell you that as the night turned to day, they made me laugh, gave me advice, covered me with their coats when the train broke down and the heater turned off. I could tell you about their struggles that they carried lightly and with grace. I could tell you that for the first time in five months, I felt connected and it was to two strangers I might never have met except for these circumstances. I was so grateful for their size because I felt I was handing over a weight so great that it required giants to hold it, if only for the short time I could bear to put it down. I will tell you that angels are sent to us all the time. They look just like ordinary people except they always tell us not to be afraid. And then, just their presence alone seems to buoy us at exactly the moment we think we are swamped.

Instead, I am going to tell you what I was wearing. I looked crazy. Crazy like someone on the street, babbling to themselves and yelling at cars. I decided to wear a track suit on the train. It was an outfit I seldom wore, even in the privacy of my own home. It was just too butt ugly. It was the color of dried mouse droppings with black, incompletely sewn stripes down the sides of the pant legs and jacket arms. The incomplete sewing had resulted in the stripes becoming skinny banners which caught the breeze and actually made sound. The suit was made of a very heavy, poly-cotton blend fleece that absorbed water like a shammy. It also smelled bad almost immediately in the best of circumstances. These were not those. Because of frequent trips to the bathroom and an aisle that had become flooded by tracked in snow, my pants were wet to the knee and incredibly heavy.

They also smelled like public restroom floor and cigarette butts. I had to keep pulling them up because the weight at the bottom threatened to "pants" me every time I moved or stood up. My face was blotchy from crying and my nose would not stop running. And still these two men took me under their wings and made sure I arrived safely in New York. Safely, but no where near on time. Thanks to snow over the tracks near Albany and a fire at Penn Station, the train arrived at a little after my job interview.

I had called my appointment several times to let her know my progress. I let her know when the train was arriving at Penn Station. This was 2003 and the Twin Towers were very fresh in everyone's minds. Penn Station, earlier in the day, had been the scene of an electrical fire. However, a fire at an area where large numbers of people congregate had to be investigated.

Thankfully, it was not terrorism but the trains were held up for hours. The huge number of people requiring taxis after trains were finally allowed back into Penn Station had caused a shortage that would take hours to work through.

In other words, getting a taxi outside of Penn Station was not going to happen. I called my interviewer to suggest that we put off our appointment to the following day. She was adamant that we try to meet that night and suggested that I walk to her hotel. I was wearing the aforementioned track suit which, after standing outside of Penn Station in ankle deep slush, had grown another two feet in length. I was going to be the first fatality due to urban drowning. Also, I hadn't really slept in 48 hours and the idea of dragging my wheeled suitcase, garment bag and briefcase through Manhattan was not lifting my mood.

I used the same fear of losing my house that drove me onto the train to spur me to walk the mile or so to the hotel where she was staying. It was really cold. It had been snowing in New York and the accumulating precipitation had immediately turned into filthy slush. And still the snow fell, melting almost immediately and soaking my already drenched track suit and my unwashed hair. She asked me how she would recognize me and I replied, "I will be the one that looks like I shouldn't be in the lobby of your hotel." She laughed a little and I assured her I wasn't kidding. I slung my briefcase and garment bag over opposing shoulders , grabbed my wheeled suitcase and began walking to the hotel. When either the garment bag or briefcase felt too heavy, I would load it onto the wheeled bag and give my shoulder a break. When the wheels of the bag got caked with snow and slush, I would drape the other bag over my shoulder, pound the snow off of the wheels and continue my trek. Unfortunately, I have no sense of direction. Fifteen minutes into my death march, I asked someone where the hotel was. They explained that I had walked in the exact wrong direction. I didn't cry. For the first time since I left Lawrence, I wasn't either on the verge of tears or actually crying. Sorrow and grief had taken a backseat to survival. I did not want to die on the streets of New York City in a mouse turd track suit. Nope. That is not how I wanted it to end.

I called my contact again to explain that I had walked in the wrong direction and would be delayed because of it but that I was certainly on my way. Just after hanging up, I stepped off of a curb, completely obfuscated by the slush and sunk up to my knee, plunging my rolling suitcase into the filthy ice. As I examined it, the zipper suddenly burst open and the entire contents, clothes, toiletries, tampons, tumbled out into the filthy water. A quick look at the bag revealed that it was not fixable.

I jammed the sodden contents back into the now useless bag and shoved it under my arm. I hung the garment bag around my neck and kept my briefcase over the other shoulder. I did not cry. It was now me against the city and I had faced greater foes than this over the past five months. I was angry now. Angry and clown-like. My already soaked pants were now three feet longer than my legs. I stopped and rolled them up but they would not stay that way. So, I tripped over them countless times on my way to the hotel. At one point, I caught a glimpse of myself in a store window. A fat, exhausted middle-aged woman glared back at me. A fat, middle-aged woman whose underwear were showing. White cotton waisties. But I was not crying. I looked insane with my hair plastered to the side of my face, bags hanging off of me like a sherpa and a track suit so filthy that I should have hung one of those air fresheners you see in cars around my neck. But I was going to that job interview. I didn't care about the results, I just didn't want to die in front of all these people looking and smelling as badly as I did. I soldiered on and arrived at the hotel a mere two hours later than our appointed time.

I was met by a well-dressed woman who had recently had her hair and make-up done. She asked me if I would like to freshen up before dinner. She offered me the use of her bathroom. It occurred to me to say, "Naw, I'm fine!" and then laugh hysterically. Instead, I went up to her room, excused myself and slipped into the tiniest bathroom I have ever seen outside of an airplane. The clothes in my rolling bag were completely soaked with New York sludge water. That meant that I would have to go with whatever I had packed in my garment bag. I also couldn't use my toothbrush. I took some toothpaste and smeared it on my teeth with my finger. All of

WEI WEI SUNFLOWER SEEDS
MARSENE FELDT

my underwear, including the ones I was wearing, were wet either from falling into the street or being worn under my wick of a track suit. I put on a pair of short pajama bottoms that bunched up immediately when I put my slacks on. I checked the mirror and was greeted with dark circles under my eyes. Fortunately, the bags were partially covering them. I noticed some makeup on the back of the toilet and dabbed some under my eyes. Somehow it made it worse but I was starting to get claustrophobic, so I called it good enough. I knew that any possibility of getting this job had been lost when she first saw me and then smelled me in the lobby. You know you are in a weird place if you hope your perspective employer is hit with the smell of train pee and cigarettes, instead of the bourbon you have been sipping on for the past 48 hours.

I stepped out of the bathroom and she asked me if I would mind walking to the restaurant. Mind?! Why would I mind? I had just walked for over an hour in a snow storm after getting no sleep for two days and drinking pretty much non-stop. I heard myself say, "No, sounds great!" This proved something I had always thought. I am an idiot. We walked the several hundred miles to the restaurant and I ordered a drink. I ordered a Manhattan. I didn't really want a Manhattan. I wanted a water glass full of bourbon, neat. I ordered and gestured to the waiter to make it a double. I wasn't sure what hand gesture you could use for a quadruple. Truthfully, I don't remember the interview. The restaurant was loud and we kept shouting "what?" at each other. I ordered another Manhattan using the same hand signal as before. There is more than one way to get a quadruple if you are motivated. Finally, the dinner was over and we walked back to her hotel. She offered to let me sleep over if I didn't want to try to get to my hotel. I would rather have relived the last 12 hours than do that so I declined. I wrapped a cord around my broken suitcase, hung my two bags from my shoulders and thanked her for her time. I assumed it would be the last time I saw her.

I went down to the street and the doorman offered to try to get me a taxi. He asked where I was going. I told him I had a hotel room across the East River in New Jersey. He

BIG BOYS DON'T CRY

Memoir of a Mid-Century Farm Boy

robertwphillips.com

A young boy's dream of becoming a cowboy meets the harsh realities of farm life, family love, and loss in this heartfelt memoir of resilience in the Kansas Flint Hills.

ROBERT W PHILLIPS

A heartwarming reminiscence of life in a small Kansas community, from a child's perspective. Experience the Kansas Flint Hills and farm life first hand. —Hugh Nicks

Robert has written a delightful memoir of his first seven years growing up as a farmer's kid in rural Kansas.The story is an accurate account of both the joys and the hardships of life on a tenant farm seventy five years ago. It was the simplicity of everyday life and love of family that brought the joy and the floods, droughts, and uncaring landlords that brought the hardships. One admires his hard working parents and sisters who created a loving, supportive home. I look forward to his second book.—Margaret Berry Culp, Classmate First three years of school,Virgil, KS

BOOK LAUNCH

Sunday, September 28, 2025, 2 to 4 pm

Union Pacific Depot (the train station in North Lawrence)

402 N 2nd St, Lawrence

told me not to tell any cab driver that I wanted to go to New Jersey. "They aren't supposed to but they won't let you in their cab if they think they have to drive way over there. Too much money in Manhattan tonight because of the fire," he explained. He said, "You're in luck though. The hotel where you are staying has a dedicated ferry. Just have the taxi take you to the ferry and it will drop you off about 20 feet from the front door of your hotel." At last my luck was turning. I would take the ferry to my hotel and, no matter what, I would sleep. I was going to finally be done with this day in a city I hated but Sue had loved. I hadn't allowed myself to think about that. About last year when we drove to New York for our very first Toy Fair. She was so excited to be here. So in love with the city and the prospects of our new business taking off. Someone had described her as "a kid in a candy store." It was impossible to think I would have her only seven more months. Impossible to think that she was gone and I was going on without her.

The doorman was able to get me a cab which took me to the port. I saw a ferry just pulling away as we drove up. I wasn't worried though. Ferries came and went. There was always another ferry. Except, as it turned out, that was the last one that went to my hotel. I would have to wait about 45 minutes for a ferry that would let me out at another port where I would need to call the hotel and they would send a bus. The fellow telling me this seemed surprised when I burst into tears. "Oh my gosh," he said, coming around the counter and putting his arm around my shoulder. "I am so sorry. Valentine's Day can be so hard when it doesn't live up to your expectations."

"It's Valentine's Day?" I cried. "Shit!"

KATHY ROBERTS. Kathy lives in the country outside of Lawrence with 3 dogs, 2 horses and one wife.

ANIMALIA (SOOTHE), BARBARA WATERMAN PETERS

PART II: POETRY

SILKEN THREADS

Poems submitted for the Summer 2025 edition of *The Write Bridge* include explorations on wind and whispers. Avoiding the void. Finding a future to believe in, and beauty where we may not have noticed it before. And knowing, as Annette Hope Billings reminds us, that it is the "poet's prerogative to not carry to term."

CELEBRATING III, BARBARA WATERMAN PETERS

How to Capture the Wind:

TA Dugan

The night brings its distance with it
& a collection of hints
skiff across the surface of her skin,
a byproduct of benefits.
& the way she moves
verges on the urge of superfluous.
But somehow,
she captures the wind.
& sends it off again
through his hair.
& she is as elusive
as the moving air.
When she says,
You can have it all.
He balks at this,
with a clinch of feelings that conflict,
with his very existence.
A Molotov cocktail in a pretty dress.
Where gas waits to be lit at its essence.
A gem on the cover dusted ashes within.
A descent down into a sarcophagus.
& all of this sounds perfect to him.
He traces the current of the wind
down the hem of her magnificence.
& says,
Who am I to contend
with how the wind behaves,
& who am I to pretend,
I could capture it,
if only for a day?

Reasons for My Discontent:
TA Dugan

A shadow behind blinded windows,
darkness that I once held easy,
plans that hesitate apart;
Now—no longer—I embrace.
A furtive smile addressed to another
with breath of whispers, I once possessed,
echoes of words lost in reflection:
I wish I knew you sooner.
I wish I never knew you.
Clash unaware of the hectic still,
in the liaison of your absence.

THADDEUS DUGAN is an American poet who is currently finishing his bachelor's degree in English at Washburn University. He is one of the editors-in-chief of Inscape, the Washburn literary journal. His debut collection, A Record of Change, came to fruition in April 2024 and is available for purchase on the Anamcara Press website. He is pleased for the opportunity to write and publish poetry. He gives all the credit to his youngest son Eliot and his youngest daughter Araya for all their support and inspiration. Non nobis solum nati sumus.

Gravid:

Annette Hope Billings

I sit splayed open watching CNN
and suspect some evening news muse
has knocked me up.
I'm rendered nauseous by thoughts of writing,
worried no good can come of this.
I am with poem.
Though it's too soon to test for what I already know,
I envision an earnest embryo intent on implantation
and in my mind's eye
I'm already beginning to show.
I ponder a poet's prerogative to not carry to term,
to bring quick end to this unplanned verse
while my first trimester is barely breached

long before quickening is felt.
I am no stranger to incubating words,
I birthed villages of verse in younger days.
But I'm older now,
weary and ill-prepared for geriatric gestation.
There is precious little of me that still dilates
with ease in these difficult times.
I suspect I could still labor
but I tremble
at what delivery would exact from me at this age.
What if even forceps fail me
leaving no option other than
I be sliced and sectioned?
Maybe I should implore some fitter poet to carry this poem,
a much stronger surrogate sounder than I.
A commercial commences on the screen
coming on loudly like a late period.
I discover, false alarm, I am not with poem at all.
I breathe relief and disappointment.

Poet that I am,
it's not pain I fear,
it is failure.

Perforation:
Annette Hope Billings

My life has had no perforated lines,

no clear instructions,
no "tear here" arrows to ease the confusion,
no notches on edges to signal
where separations should start.
My life had always been just my best guess,
my eyeballed estimation of
what I hoped was most correct.
It's been scarce on learned guidance
or expert direction about what to discard
or what to keep.
I have not been granted time
to measure twice and cut once,
so, I've applied scissors and sheared
through this journey as precisely as I could.
I'm afraid I've closed my eyes
and just let life rip at times
without sufficient planning.
I believe I've lived as true as I could
with what I've known
but I may have mismeasured.
I am sorry,
I've never had any perforated lines.

ANNETTE HOPE BILLINGS is an award-winning poet known for the impact of her audible presentations of work. In 2015 she brought her registered nursing career to an early end to fully pursue her passion for writing. That same year her first collection of poetry, *A Net Full of Hope*, received Topeka's ARTSConnect's ARTY Award in Literature. Her second and third books, Descants for a Daughter and Just Shy of Stars followed. Billings' work, including prose and short stories, can also be found in a variety of anthologies as well as in print and online journals.

One of the events she values most is the monthly open mic in its tenth year, First Wednesday Speak Easy Poets Topeka, KS, which she co-hosts with fellow poet Sue Edgerton-Johnston.

Crystal Blue:
Hannah Corynne Caycedo

The feeling settles, nothing new,
My mind spins a dizzying hue.
Velvet night drapes thick and deep,
Its shadows closing, swallowing me.
The stars are distant, pale and stark,
Cold and faded, a dying spark.
And that old stillness, vast and deep,
Slides in slow where sorrow sleeps.
Alone, I stare with hollow view,
Its beauty stark, but built for two
And yet it waits for what's not there—
For someone else to breathe the air.
And so, I dive into the crystal water,
A midnight plunge, a lover's slaughter
The icy depths, like glass, unfold,
Their silent grip both dark and cold.
The stars above, a fractured gleam,
Blur in waves, dissolve in stream,
While shadows curl in cascading grace,
To pull me to their hollowed place.
I sink beneath, in whispered thrall,
Where secrets drift and voices call.
The world above, a ghostly shore,
Where dreams return to me no more.
Through shadowed depths, I slip unseen,
A phantom lost in twilight's sheen—
For here, alone, the world is true,
A crystal grave for lovers two.

The Void:

Hannah Corynne Caycedo

In twilight's grip both dark and sheer,
A whisper called, "Come near, come near."
The cliff, a shadowed, ghostly pier,
Drew me, entranced, to venture near.
The air was thick with haunting sound,
A pull so deep, my soul unwound.
"Step closer now," its calls resound,
My legs are weak and feet are bound.
"Closer,"
My mind is spinning now,
I can feel its' spell, a whispered vow
"Come closer,"
A pitch, I'm falling now,
And yet, alas my feet are ground.
"The edge,"
The wind is whipping 'round,
My heart is racing, I'm hurtling down
"You're falling."
Yes, a roaring sound,
My eyes are closing, impact, now
They open,
My feet are firmly ground
"You don't wonder?"
Yes, I wonder now.

HANNAH CORYNNE CAYCEDO is a writer exploring dark, mysterious themes of beauty, terror, love, and desolation; she is inspired by Edgar Allen Poe and philosophers like Kant and Burke.

we are all the fish on the hook:

Iris Craver

Innocently going about the daily goings on of living life, making a cup of coffee, running to the store for bread, showing up for work, calling the kids, doing the wash, the seemingly mundane. Caught. Wiggle this way. Wiggle that way. Painful. Acting like its all ok.

A Future to Believe In:
Iris Craver

The wind is blowing dust in the air and I still dare to believe in a future.
Where my grandbabies can know the beauty of our world.
And love is unfurled,
Not hate.
Where we all have a place at the table.
And build bridges, not walls,
After all.
Where education is free and war is no more and the water is clean and food is real food and there's a guaranteed income and work is not wage slavery and we take care of our elders and everyone has a decent place to live and we treat what ails rather than sending to jail and health care is a right.
I dream of this at night.

IRIS CRAVER is living a life in North Lawrence, Kansas between the tracks and the river. She and her husband, Steve Stemmerman, enjoy working in a very large garden, spending time with family and friends, and traveling. Her publications include *Do Lizards Have Lips? And Other Tall Tales From Toronto, Kansas, Spice it Up! An Herbal Extravaganza* and *Write to the Source ~ A Journaling Guide for Recovery.*

17 Magazine:

Beth Gulley

In the high school library,
we scour back issues of 17 Magazine
instead of reading Shakespeare.
The glossy pages show
tall thin girls walking through Paris
or running on the beach.
They never speak.
They never get rejected.
They never have cellulite.
If we had bothered
with Shakespeare
we would have noticed
all the lines for girls
were intended to be
said by men.
The love-struck Juliet,
the weak Ofelia
would later be reimagined
to match twenty first century
thoughts about women,
but in 1991
we were 17-year-old girls
looking for ideals
but forging our own way.

BETH GULLEY was an Amity literary prize finalist in 2023. The contest is sponsored by Anamcara Press. Beth Gulley lives in Spring Hill, Kansas and teaches writing at Johnson County Community College. She has published two chapbooks and three full-length collections of poetry: *Since Corona Ruined Our Trip to the Library* (Finishing Line Press), *Little Fish: Tiny Meditations on Freedom* (Flying Ketchup Press), *Dragon Eggs* (Spartan Press), *The Sticky Note Alphabet* (Alien Buddha Press), and *Love of Ornamental Fish* (Alien Buddha). Beth serves on the Riverfront Reading Committee and is a Writer's Place board member where she edits the yearbook. More information about Beth can be found on her blog at https://timeeasesallthings.wordpress.com/.

KLINT THE SWAN, MARSENE FELDT

Painting:

Barbara Waterman-Peters

I covered the rock of ancient caves, told the story of mystic hunts,
graced the walls of plundered tombs, witnessed Pompeii's violent doom.
Books of Hours, scrolls of lamb, woven reed, colors bright, with henna and gall,
recorded prayer and bravest deed, saved for human need or soul.

Wooden panel, plastered wall, priceless scenes of life and myth, told well, told all,
brilliant hues, magic forms, wonders press against the eye—light in darkest hall.
Images speak of the scourge of God's wrath, the strength and terror of Zeus.
Lessons on the spiritual path, for those whose morals are somewhat loose.

Susannah, Diana, Potiphar's wife, they all look great on my canvas.
Tales and woes and those of the elders, cover my surface in large masses.
Troubles and labor of a peasant, poverty, famine, wars and the plague,
with others just as unpleasant. Strange, the things for which they are paid.

Portraits abound of kings and their queens, cloth of gold, and starchy lace,
bejeweled necklaces, diamond rings, and every conceivable face.
My creators limn emperors, too: Napolean's glory David shows.
Gainsborough mocks Reynolds with Boy Blue, Van Gogh ends with crows.

I am PAINTING; I am not dead yet, though my breath is weak as the isms crowd
around my bed, hedging their bets, wringing their hands, pulling up my shroud.
Ab Ex, Surreal, Magic, and Post, my meaning is lost in Kant's theory that painting
is flat, and at the most, an overdue death, lifeless and weary.

But watch out for me I'm on the rise! I'm better than ever with Kiefer, Nerdrum,
and Kowch. It's no surprise! Mitchell, Saville, and Flack—artists like them!
I'm coming through darkness into light, the human condition ever new
entices artists to take up the fight to give me my hierarchical due!

BARBARA WATERMAN-PETERS, (BFA, Washburn University, MFA, Kansas State University, Honorary Doctor of Fine Arts, Washburn University) taught at Washburn and Kansas State Universities as well as for Lassen Community College in California. She has received a Certificate of Recognition for Outstanding Achievement from the State of Kansas and the Monroe Award from the Washburn University Alumni Association. In 2011 she was awarded the ARTY for Distinguished Visual Artist from ARTS Connect in Topeka. Her work has been included in more than 300 solo, group and juried exhibits. She is represented by several galleries, Jones in Kansas City, SNW in Manhattan, and Beauchamp in Topeka. She owns STUDIO 831 in the North Topeka Arts & Entertainment District (NOTO).

Barbara Waterman-Peters' poems are in 150kansaspoems.com, Kansas Speaks Out, The Writers Place Yearbooks, All Over the Map: An Anthology, The Write Bridge, The Love Book.

Almost Too Late:

Julie Ann Baker Brin

You realize suddenly your Mother was
gorgeous. That never really
mattered—and it still doesn't,
really, but it's something
perhaps you should have
seen sooner. Of course, as a kid you were
too busy looking at yourself. In the mirror,
in pictures, in plate glass windows. So many
hours collected and wasted—they would end
up in an estate auction if tangible. Not true
memories to keep. Not genuine
reflection.

Lumiere:

Julie Ann Baker Brin

I don't mind electric candles
nor a gas fireplace
or any attempt to contain
something so wild
The flickers catch me
all the same, draw me
in, keep me warm,
guide my way
The illumination is not
an illusion—
the light is still
so vital, so real

By day, JULIE ANN BAKER BRIN works in broadcasting: not behind a mic, but behind red tape. By night, she prefers to use the other brain hemisphere. She's an award-winning Kansas Authors Club member. JulieBrin.org showcases her works from *105 Meadowlark Reader*, Flying Ketchup's *Night Forest*, WSU's *Mikrokosmos* and more. Julie is the winner of the 2024 Amity Literary Award offered by Anamcara Press.

Sense Divine:

Boyd Bauman

Orient yourself:
Shinshoji Zen Buddhist temple,
Eastern Hiroshima Prefecture,
Friday night of a weekend retreat.
A small group of gaijin
are led by a monk
to a meditation hall
at the edge of a bamboo forest.

Center your being:
zazen on the wooden porch,
peering into the unknown depths
of the dark forest shadow play.

Inhale:
rain traipsing on the awning above
invokes every cypress plank
from the ancient wooden complex
to exude a sweet sylvan smell
that dances with the incense burning within
through acute olfactory to synapses
on the cusp of perceiving a wisp
of the esoteric divine.

Awaken:
By the glare of the following morning,
the master verbalizes the lessons:
The world is illusion
where senses deceive.

Empty yourselves,
embrace nothing but the absence
of the divine.

Meditate on this:
All these years later, rain still awakens me,
summons me to a wooden porch
where I breath in the mixture
of memory and mystery
this fair earth exudes,
my muddy conduit to divine.

All these years later,
I'm still in love
with something I can only sense.

BOYD BAUMAN grew up on a small ranch south of Bern, Kansas, his dad the storyteller and mom the family scribe. His books of poetry are Cleave and Scheherazade Plays the Chestnut Tree Café, and his children's book is The Heights of Love. After stints in New York, Colorado, Alaska, Japan, and Vietnam, Boyd now is a librarian and writer in Kansas City. Visit at boydbauman.weebly.com.

Concupiscence:
Bruce Rolfe

I took a drive down an older highway
that had been paved over twice before.
Its untried, yet familiar hills and curves
lured me a thousand miles,
before I pulled over and looked back
at the many scenic straightaways
I'd hardly noticed coming through.
Because of several potholes
that no amount of asphalt could patch,
I'd missed the joys of driving
worrying about my car.

Virga:
Bruce Rolfe

Rain evaporates
not quenching parched soil; nature
sheds crocodile tears.

BRUCE ROLFE, a former U.S. Navy Search & Rescue pilot for 20 years, is proud to say there are nine souls here today because he was there then. He is the author of the Chip Hale handyman series of mystery novels, *Tools of the Trade, Trademark of Murder*, and *Trade Secrets*. His next book, *Family Trade* is forthcoming. Bruce also has a new standalone book coming out from Dingbat Publishing. *The Little Storehouse in the Middle of the Block* is the memoir of a wannabe writer, who at 47, discovered after his mother's death that he was adopted, she was murdered, and his quest to find his biological parents. Find Bruce here: http://brucerolfe.com/

Scan for a good time!

Shoe String Memories:

JA McGovern

In short:
All that matters—are the shoe string memories,
We learn to tie…
And the ones, we forgot to untie.

J.A. MCGOVERN is a published poet, songwriter, and independent filmmaker. "Words Left Unspoken" is J.A. McGovern's first poetry collection publication. McGovern was an Amity literary prize finalist in 2023. The contest is sponsored by Anamcara Press. A graduate, with a bachelor's degree in forensic science - chemistry focus with criminal justice minor, J.A. McGovern currently works as an analytical inorganic chemist. Founder and curator of the literary art anthology "Perception" his artistic team has received multiple nominations and awards for their work. In 2018, J.A. McGovern received an American Songwriting Award for lyrics in folk music, for his independent film's title song, "All Over Again."

The Three Sisters:
Craig Sweets

Three Women imply a slightly
sisterly set of powers; three
men, a coherent clan, a brotherhood.

But to the Mississippian Indians,
the "three sisters" were corn, squash, and beans.
Mom and I trekked up Monk's Mound,
whereupon I thought I heard the sound
of a pan flute in the near distance.
From the top, I flung back a glance
on Cahokia's mounds, and at their fringe,
the majestic arc of Woodhenge,
where aeons before, natives danced a Sundance.

Cahokia was a rich and populous nation;
with bird man's flutes and tambourines,
and the three sisters, corn and squash and beans,
theirs was another incantation
from the gold-hungry Spanish and their cruel spite.

Early one morning or evening you might
catch bright Venus or the ruddy crest of Mars,
or, in the neighborhood of stars,
chance to see a triad of sisters,
which above Monk's Mound glisters.

Summer:
Craig Sweets

The hot season is already here,
the torrid time of year.
Toiling in the early summer sun,
there's plenty of work to be done.
I am only an amateur,
often don't know a weed from a flower.
The iris, lilac, and peony,
I know these by color and by smell,
but what I know in bloom,
I do not know in bud.

Creatures from a long-ago flood—
the slow slug, the sluggish snail—
make their way along a cool mud trail.
Frank is nearly eighty-three now,
working by the sweat of his brow.
As an apprentice, for seven years under Frank,
I have learned much, have him to thank
for what to water, trim, and leave alone.
It takes gardeners years to hone
their skill. Poets, too, need to learn
what to add, and what to leave alone.

When he's not writing, CRAIG SWEETS works at the Audio-Reader Sensory Garden (on campus) is the founding editor of *Change of Heart*, a streetpaper for and by homeless people in Lawrence and Douglas County for over twenty years. Other interests include classical music, visiting alpaca farms, and local history (e.g.: the Underground Railroad).

The Darkness:
Brian Daldorph

When I was a boy,
I couldn't resist
going out to that quarry pit,
past all the red DANGER signs.
I'd wriggle in through holes
in the barbed wire fence.
At dusk I'd feel the night
spreading outside and in me,
and I wanted it to fill me up.
I had cigarettes, vodka,
a thousand songs in my head.
I'd sit at the edge
of Death's Head Cliff,
and it wasn't Smirnoff or Marlboro
that flooded my head,
it was the darkness rushing into me
as though I'd heard my calling:
a few inches away from death
was exactly where I should be.

BRIAN DALDORPH teaches at the University of Kansas and Douglas County Jail. He edits *Coal City Review*. His most recent books of poetry are *Ice Age/ Edad de Hielo* (Irrupciones P, 2017), *Blue Notes* (Dionysia P, 2019), and *Kansas Poems* (Meadowlark P, 2021).

[evergreen swinging]:
Kerry Moyer & Kevin Rabas

As a kid, age 8, I put my hands
on the evergreen limbs
and lifted, and the tree's
sap clung to my skin
in blotches, and would hardly
come off. I scraped knees
and elbows on the bark,
and grew tall. Together,
the tree and I lifted up
towards the sun, but rooted
we held on, until I grew older
and no longer clung and swung
in those branches, but never
forgot the sticky balm of youth.

[balloon animals]:
Kerry Moyer & Kevin Rabas

The big plastic letters of TG &_ flickered red
above, Dad in his clown costume: big floppy blue shoes,
gigantic Chuck Taylors, red-orange wig, one eye with a
colored
patch around it, like the Lil' Rascals dog, and he's
blowing up
and tying off balloon animals, no kids there, no kids
yet, and mom and brother and I show up and watch, wait,
and a kid comes with his mom, and the kid wants a
balloon,
and dad pulls a goofy face, asks the kid what he wants,
says,
"You want a dog?" and the kid nods, and dad bends the
balloon
half a dozen times, hands the kid a red balloon dog,
and the mom says, "Tell the man thank you," and he does,
and dad goes back to looking sad. Under
those fluorescent lights something felt wrong—
twisted, broken, like a balloon busted, a husk.

KERRY MOYER is the author of three collections of poetry from Kellogg Press. They are 2019's release *Dirt Road,* 2020's *Rust & Weeds* and 2021's Turnpike Prairie. Moyer writes about rural life, the Flint Hills of east central Kansas, gravel cycling, his struggles, passions, musings and whatever serves to inspire his craft. Moyer resides in Emporia, Kan., with his wife Sarah and their boys Edward and Miles.

KEVIN RABAS, http://kevinrabas.com/ Past Poet Laureate of Kansas (2017-2019) Kevin Rabas teaches at Emporia State University, where he leads the poetry and playwriting tracks in the Department of English, Modern Languages, and Journalism. He is a seventh generation Kansan. He has fourteen books, including *Lisa's Flying Electric Piano,* a Kansas Notable Book and Nelson Poetry Book Award winner. He is the recipient of the Emporia State President's and Liberal Arts & Sciences Awards for Research and Creativity, and he is the winner of the Langston Hughes Award for Poetry.

Processed Meats, Bitch:

Amber Fraley

I see you turkey sandwich,
chiding me from the menu
You should pick me! Make good choices!
think of your weight and your heart!

I have ordered and consumed many
turkey sandwiches,
Lovely things that tasted
of angels and arugula
and cranberrries and sprouts

And my heart did sing and rejoice
And my arteries thanked m'lady for treating us nice

But lately I've been pretending I don't know who they
are, my heart and arteries,
And I've given myself over to
salami, and prosciutto and pancetta and spicy mr.
capicola and it is

So delicious. So enticing.

Garlic, paprika, onion, pepper, salt, salt, SALT

processed meats, Bitch

They are the cocaine of meat
The heroin of meat

And my big boned Midwestern
Genes originally from
The land of processed meats
Sausages, frankfurters, bratwurst, mortadella, pancetta,
kielbasa

Cry out for those indecent,
Fatty, organ based Franken-meats
and I am

Powerless
to say no.

AMBER FRALEY is a native Kansan, journalist, essayist, storyteller, and wife and mom to the two greatest people in the world. She's the author of the darkly humorous essay collection *From Kansas, Not Dorothy*, and the viral essay *Gen X Will Not Go Quietly,* as well as numerous human-interest articles in regional magazines like KANSAS!. Growing up in Lawrence and Wichita, Amber spent her formative years with her face in a book or at the mall with her friends. She loves the Kansas with all her heart, is frequently awkward in public, and desperately wishes to see a tornado and live to tell the tale.

CREEPY CAMPANILE, CATHY MARTIN

PART III: TALL TALES, SHORT STORIES & ONE ACT PLAYS

YARNS

Fiction submitted for the Summer 2025 edition of *The Write Bridge* explores ideal spaces and what happens when we leave them, in Lesa F. Robert's "Home." Unexpected messages that arrive just at the right time, in Bruce Rolfe's "Coffees With The Lord." A near-miss in Ralvell Rogers', "KC Superman." And the illumination that comes from stepping outside your own skin, in "Scrubs." And more.

Connlyn Sinclair in "Orestes Meets Cryptic Jack" reminds us there is "much to be learned from the study of illusion."

SUN AND SONG, KENT SMITH

Orestes Meets Cryptic Jack:
Connlyn Sinclair

Suburbia is active at night. It's a fact that makes some uncomfortable, but late night living is a hard habit for humanity to break. There were of course the high-class dinner parties where jars of wine were passed around, and movie clubs too, but things happened outdoors at the same time. Moonlit yard sales catered to those who worked long hours, and lanterns illuminated late night basketball games between hustlers.

Of course, the shadows were a boon to those with less than honorable intentions, so journalist Johnny Orestes tried to find excuses to do some late night activities for the chance to find interesting stories.

Johnny had just been at a yard sale hosted by an apartment complex. Some young wheeler-dealer was selling vintage trading cards for $50 apiece, but was letting a CD-rom of magic tricks go for $5.70.

Johnny couldn't help but laugh as he walked to the next yard sale on his list. There was much to be learned from the study of illusion, while the value of a trading card was only in nostalgia.

Porch lights illuminated the path and Johnny could see a young woman selling cups of tea up ahead. The night might be liberating but it was still chilly.

"Good evening. You're very brave to be manning a lone stall in the darkness. I hope you're carrying a baseball bat at least." Johnny took out his wallet and looked over the menu.

"Oh? You a watchmen?" the young woman asked.

"No I'm a reporter lamenting the fact there's no mischief to grab on my camera. I'll take a wild herb."

The young woman got to work making his tea. A group of young men exited a nearby house. They were all college age with scruffy beards, loose fitting t-shirts and sandals. The young woman gave them a dirty look.

Johnny wasn't paying as much attention as he should have been to what happened next.

A figure in a long coat glided down the street without walking. It had glowing yellow eyes, unnaturally long fingers and laughed as it went by with a loud whooping sound. It was the very image of an old-school urban ghost. In its hand was an axe that dripped with what looked like someone's fresh blood.

"It killed Rufus! That fiend!" Came a cry from the house to the right of the tea stand. An old man ran out holding a dead dog. A large knife was embedded in its head.

The young men in unison ran over to look at the corpse, while the barista crossed herself and said something under her breath. Johnny did neither. No, he played the scene back again in his mind.

"It was Cryptid Jack! To think I saw him once again before I died! Oh God, why? Why has he taken my poor Rufus from me!?" The man continued, but Johnny couldn't help but laugh at his bad acting.

Suddenly the eyes of the entire crowd had settled on Johnny. He walked over to where 'Cryptid Jack' had been standing a moment earlier.

"I'm sorry. I didn't mean to be rude, it's just this isn't actually my first encounter with Cryptid Jack. There was a man on Cody Street who was stabbed by Cryptid Jack—except it turned out to be his daughter-in-law wearing heavy makeup and an electrician's jumpsuit." He paused for a moment to kneel down and examine the ground.

"The daughter-in-law had gotten the idea from the time Cryptid Jack stole a motorcycle from a policeman. In that instance, it turned out to be a clown who was promoting a TV show and the policeman had also been an actor."

"Simply put, Cryptid Jack doesn't exist. Perhaps he did once, but crimes committed by madmen or copycats can create the illusion of a pattern and that pattern creates further copycats therefore the myth will never die." Johnny finished.

The group of young men whispered amongst themselves for a moment. Johnny could see that they were still frightened, despite his words. Well, it made sense; ghost or human, it

WATERMARK BOOKS & CAFE
BOOKS

had senselessly murdered the dog. At least that was the logical inference from what they had seen.

"If you don't believe me come over here and look."

Each of the young men took a step backwards, but the barista came with Johnny's cup of tea in hand.

"Okay, look at what?" she asked. Her voice was stern—there was certainly a challenge there.

Johnny turned on his phone's light.

"No blood. Now think back to what we saw. There was an axe dripping with blood right? So where's the blood?"

The Barista touched the ground.

"It's wet."

"But blood is sticky and would stain the ground red. Besides we're missing the obvious. There's a knife in the dog's body but the ghost had an axe."

Johnny took out his wallet to pay for the tea, but the Barista stopped him. He tipped his hat, took a sip of the tea and then pointed to the old man.

"Clearly this is a hoax set up by you. After all, it's your dog who's dead and you who said the words 'Cryptid Jack'. I'm going to call the ASPCA in the morning, and you need to have a good explanation about your dog. I'd suggest coming up with a better defense than an urban legend."

The old man said nothing. He simply dropped the dog's corpse and retreated back into his house.

"Man, you're stupid. I know what I saw," one of the young men said.

"Yeah, I've read a little parapsychology and life persists after death man. Cryptid Jack is the real deal," added another.

The group dispersed and went their separate ways into the night while Johnny watched curiously.

"I think you can explain the last part of this mystery," Johnny said at last.

"What?" The barista shifted nervously.

"I can guess most of the actual illusion: Reflective sunglasses and roller blades, probably. But I don't have a motive. Why?"

"Will you leave my name out of it?"

"Scout's honor. You are an anonymous source," Johnny confirmed.

"Those guys? They're all big into fantasy role-playing games. Old man Nestor thinks they're all losers and has lamented that Congress repealed the draft. Nestor has also said that if the supernatural became real and tangible to them they might turn to god and get their act together."

"Old man Nestor as in Sapperstein Nestor the film producer?" Johnny frowned. He'd seen several of the old man's films. It made sense now; the whole thing had been managed like the cuts of a movie.

He handed the barista a twenty and she glanced at it curiously.

"For the first cup of tea. And you know what? I'll take another. Whatever's left is a tip. I gotta run."

This time it was the barista's turn to laugh.

CONNLYN SINCLAIR published his first story, ***a Pastiche of Ovid***, in a high school literary journal at 17. Since then he has written a number of stories inspired by mythology and classic literature many of which have appeared in *The Kraken Lore.* His children's novel ***Young Robin Hood*** was recently published by Anamcara Press.

Home:

Lesa F. Roberts

It sits on a corner lot—its architecture reflects a prescriptive design. A new house—unoccupied for five years. Strollers push and wagons pull past this house heading to the park. Dogs walk in heat and wind and snow—waste scooped from an apathetic yard. Only rumors explain this lonely landmark.

It deteriorates. Blades disappear from the patio fan—it dangles crookedly from its base. The outdoor fireplace hemorrhages dirty insulation from its broken frame. Snowy funnel shaped bindweed flowers choke glossy-leafed bushes. Rain gutters empty into deepening ruts.

A *For Sale* placard appears. An S.O.S. signal—or defeat.

Homes thrum with the din of visitors. Laughter of friends and family. Raucous noise of holidays. Crabby children fighting and shouting. All that pushing and shoving and noise contained. Homes witness who we've been and who we've become. New babies. Old dog. An office sanctuary. A door to slam. Shielding tears when love leaves. Dreams perish. They lull us to sleep with settling sighs—aging creaks and moans. They occupy us—upkeep calming our restless souls.

Moving out of a house, look around into the void you've created. It may gasp at you, urging you back. Shed tears. Your gut may tighten. Is this the right decision? Your brain registers emptiness—the ceiling, the lights, the blank walls. There's that carpet stain.

He trembled on his four paws—barely able to stand. It was time. A bedroom painted dove beige. Against your better judgment—a floral border. Parts of you occupy the emptiness. Close and lock the door. Pack your memories.

Doubt and regret may ring back, clattering like a dropped pot. A new house cannot be responsible for your grievances. Refuge, solace, and liberation may come quickly or achingly slow. First reside—then live anew.

At the corner house, healthy boxwoods are weeded and mulched. They usher visitors to the front door. An SUV sporting a nubby-tired bicycle on its rack is in the garage. A lush lawn is neatly edged and mulched—trees added to the backyard. There is a new ceiling fan and a teakwood settee and chair on the patio. An elderly man, his legs crossed at the ankles, sits in the teakwood chair reading in the comfort of his home.

LESA F. ROBERTS, nurse and public health administrator for 44 years, retired to care for her granddaughter. And with her muse at her side (and in her arms), she began writing again. Her poetry was published by a national women's magazine while in nursing school, but over the years her priorities shifted. She grew her career in public health, raised a daughter, managed a home and houseful of pets in addition to competing as a runner, swimmer, and triathlete. Lesa writes poetry and essays through a prism of humor and an understanding of human nature and the natural world. Her current project is a novel about a marathon runner who goes missing. Lesa and her spouse, Rick Beattie, live in Lawrence.

“Coffees with the Lord”: Bruce Rolfe

Each morning I leave my trailer with coffee in hand and trudge out an old gravel road, not yet fully awake. My aging black lab runs ahead and I can see our breath–fleeting puffs in the crisp, cold air. The high desert is particularly beautiful as I stop in front of a small scrub-covered knoll and talk with my maker. It is the hill where I discovered that the Lord lives. At least it’s where I’ve found him most often. A non-pretentious scrub-covered knoll surrounded in the distance by majestic mountains, anyone of which would be much more suited to His countenance. Nevertheless, I believe the Lord in his awesome wisdom knows it is easier for us to approach Him at our level. Yet, who would think to look in so humble a place?

I’m not sure exactly why I first stopped in front of that insignificant knoll, but a friend was dying from stage-four, terminal cancer and I paused briefly to ask the Lord to watch over him. Not necessarily to let him live as I so desperately wanted, but to do what was best for him.

At about that time, *Jeep* was running a TV commercial that showed two huge hands scooping mounds of dirt together forming what looked like mountains. As the hands opened for the third time, birds flew out and a mountain lion leaped onto the newly formed peaks. The fingers of one hand drummed on the ground and a puzzled “Uhm,” descended from the clouds, A moment later the other hand set a Jeep Grand Cherokee on the hillside and, as it drove away, the next exclamation sounded pleased. “Aha.”

I’m sure the Lord could have chosen a burning bush or any number of showy responses to my prayer, however I knew that my prayer was answered simply and immediately with a touch of humor. I just didn’t know how; but had to smile as a white Jeep CJ-4 came over the hill.

Although I'm not foolish enough to believe the Lord was driving, I do believe he had a hand with it coming over that inconsequential hillside at that precise moment.

Today, several years later, my friend is still alive. Coffees with the Lord are a great way to start the day giving thanks for being alive and open to His signs.

BRUCE ROLFE, a former U.S. Navy Search & Rescue pilot for 20 years, is proud to say there are nine souls here today because he was there then. He is the author of the Chip Hale handyman series of mystery novels, *Tools of the Trade, Trademark of Murder*, and *Trade Secrets*. His next book, *Family Trade* is forthcoming. Bruce also has a new standalone book coming out from Dingbat Publishing. *The Little Storehouse in the Middle of the Block* is the memoir of a wannabe writer, who at 47, discovered after his mother's death that he was adopted, she was murdered, and his quest to find his biological parents. Find Bruce here: http://brucerolfe.com/

The Strong Man:
Brian Daldorph

At rallies they shake my hand: "Keep us safe, General. Keep us safe and we will love you. We don't care how you do it. Do what's necessary."

They're scared of guerilla fighters who'd kill them and help themselves to everything, who'd carry off their women and children. They believe that I'm the only one who can stop them.

"I am your humble servant," I tell the huge crowd. "I will do what you bid me to do."

I send my troops into the jungle to root out insurgents, to destroy their camps and training grounds, but my soldiers are peasants, stupid and poorly equipped. Some of them desert and slide back to their villages, some of them are so scared they kill anyone they come across and help themselves to the spoils of war.

Most of the time I keep the insurgents out of our towns and cities and my people cheer me and say, "You are a strong man, General. We need your strength."

But there's this burning in my stomach again after I eat even the blandest food, and the dizziness at night, especially when I'm tired. My doctor says I must have an operation: "Most men are up from it in a few days." He thinks I will be displeased if he gives me bad news.

Reports of a suicide bombing in a southern city. An attack on a police headquarters in the East. My minister of defense funneling government money into his own accounts.

My mistress telling me her husband beats her and what am I supposed to do about that?

BRIAN DALDORPH teaches at the University of Kansas and Douglas County Jail. He edits ***Coal City Review.*** His most recent books of poetry are *Ice Age/ Edad de Hielo* (Irrupciones P, 2017), *Blue Notes* (Dionysia P, 2019), and *Kansas Poems* (Meadowlark P, 2021).

Scrubs:
M Carroll

Tisha escorted Grace into the university hospital's emergency waiting room. The sun was going down and red-orange streaks painted the horizon. *For Godsakes it's already evening.*

"I've missed my hair appointment." Grace touched her head and felt soft, shoulder-length curls.

She followed Tisha dutifully, dazed.

"Sit."

Grace did as she was told. Squirming on a plastic chair clearly designed to be uncomfortable. It was attached to the chair next to it, inflexible. Just like her life was inflexible. Everything lined up right in a row and fixed. A life of boring repetition and sameness—until now.

The room was overflowing with people in various forms of misery. The man next to her coughed—wet and deep-throated and likely contagious. Grace leaned away from him and waited—for what she was not sure—with Tisha beside her reading a *Popular Mechanic's* magazine.

The receptionist returned the laminated ID cards from the cartoon-cat covered wallet in the green velvet purse found in locker #101.

"You do not have to stay," Grace said again, she continued to stare at her blue finger nails.

"I do need to stay until they take you back," Tisha didn't look up from the magazine.

"I am not crazy," Grace repeated, more to herself than to Tisha.

"Um hmm."

The hospital was busy and time passed slowly. Grace talked herself into and out of leaving, twice, before a young woman in scrubs announced, "Megan O'Neal." The name meant nothing to Grace and she continued staring at her nails.

"Megan O'Neal?"

"That's you," Tisha practically lifted Grace from the chair by her elbow. Grace followed the woman in scrubs but looked back at Tisha, wishing she were staying by her side. It felt right to have a woman of strength nearby while she confronted this ... insanity.

"Let's get some vitals, shall we?" Grace followed the woman in scrub's directions and stepped up onto a scale. "One hundred and thirty pounds; five foot seven inches."

She was led into a small room and directed to sit on a paper-covered raised platform. "Blood pressure normal. Can you tell me what's brought you here today?" the woman in scrubs asked while typing into an electronic notebook.

"Uh, I guess you could say I'm not myself," Grace laughed, a strange inappropriate laugh, she thought. The woman in scrubs looked up.

"Did you have an accident?"

"I almost drowned. But when they revived me, I was not at the Monterey. I was at a different pool."

The woman in scrubs decided to read her notes. "You think you're ... someone else?" She asked hesitantly.

"No. I think I'm myself in someone else's body."

"... You're ... Megan O'Neal ...?"

"No. I'm Grace Browne. I live in the Upper East Side. I really must call my husband. I'm certain he'll want to be here, pick me up, figure out what is going on."

The green velvet purse with tassels and the grimy gym bag sat on a plastic chair nearby. "Is your phone in there?" Scrubs pointed to the green purse and Grace looked inside. There was the cartoon-cat covered wallet, a paperback novel—*Lord of the Flies*, a set of keys on a leather fob, a pocket knife, a mini-flashlight, a notepad with what looked like a lot of math notes inside, several pens and pencils, hand cream, a purple crystal on a chain, hard candy, and crumpled receipts and loose tissues—maybe clean. No phone. As she looked through the green purse, the gym bag buzzed. The phone was in there.

Grace dug out the phone with some trouble, unzipping three zippers before she found the vibrating device. "Hello?"

"Megan?" There was a long pause following.

"No. This is not Megan. Who is this?" A soft click let her know the caller had disconnected.

Grace held a stranger's phone in her hand—luckily it was unlocked, hers had facial recognition—and started to dial Phillip's cell but then she couldn't remember the last four digits.

"His number is on speed dial but I don't ..."

"I'll be right back," Scrubs announced.

Grace tried several phone numbers, hanging up twice on unfamiliar "Hello's." Finally, Phillip answered.

"Thank God. You need to come pick me up right away. For Godssakes, where am I?" She looked frantically around the small hospital admitting room. "University Hospital on Clarkson in Brooklyn. That's it. How soon can you get here?"

There was a long pause. Grace thought he'd hung up.

"Who is this?"

"What do you mean who is this? I'm at my wits end, Phillip. You need to pick me up right away!" She thought she heard a voice in the background ask inquisitively. "Phil?"

"You must have the wrong number."

The phone went silent.

Grace called again immediately. This time there was no answer. She waited for the message tone, tapping her foot, and left a frantic message, then pressed redial once, twice, three times ...

Grace wasn't sure how things got out of control. Scrubs had come into the tiny room while Grace was screaming into the phone, "Phillip! Answer this phone this minute! You idiot!"

Scrubs was flanked by the Rock on one side and the Hulk on the other, both wearing green hospital garb. They tried unsuccessfully to get Grace to sit down in a wheel chair. Finally, they lifted her up with rough hands and stuffed her into the chair, securing straps around her wrists and ankles. Scrubs sank a needle into her arm painfully. She awoke strapped to a hard mattress flat on her back in a different tiny room. She screamed for help until she was hoarse. No one came.

This excerpt is from the soon-to-be-released Sci Fi Comedy-thriller, *Just One Second: Switched and Enriched.*

M Carroll is a writer, educator, photographer, graphic designer, and all around cat herder! Her first book, *A Wyoming Cowboy in Hitler's Germany* Combines war era correspondence and 70 year old photographs to depict an age of heroism and innocence. *The Tree Who Walked Through Time* was published in collaboration with 17 artists, including crop artist Stan Herd. Carroll has also published several children's books, and many non-fiction articles & training programs, and blogs about consciousness and community at https://maureencarroll.com/.

Two Brothers, Hood Heroes, KC Superman & Jesus:

Ralvell Rogers

"Nave, please take off the cape, man. You're embarrassing me, and you look dusty."

"Why?" Nave hopped down from the black monkey bars and stepped in front of Gideon, who tightened the knot on his royal blue satin durag. "And how? We're the only ones out here." Nave placed his hands on his hips in his best Captain Underpants pose. It wasn't too bad either. His red cape glided on top of the wind.

"Stop being such a meanie-butt, Gideon," Nave added. "It's really bringing me down."

The sun pierced into Gideon's right eye, so he shielded his face with his hand while still trying to look at Nave. "Oh, I'm bringing you down now? And come on with that kiddie talk, man. I told you about that." Gideon squinted his eyes even though the shadow from his hand was blocking the sun. "You're officially going to be in sixth grade by the end of the summer. It's time to cut that 'meanie-butt' business out, lil bro."

"Yeah yeah yeah. Are you bout to give me the 'it's time to be a man speech?' I'll have you know that Daddy already beat you to it after we all got back from seeing *Infinity Wars*... three weeks ago."

He held up three fingers as if to say, *so get out of my business meanie-butt,* and ran to climb the orange ladder leading to the slide.

"Speaking of the Avengers," Gideon lowered his eyes with mild concern. "I'm actually glad you brought it up, cuz I've been meaning to talk to you about your little obsession with Marvel."

"Oh yeah?" Nave had reached the top of the long tan slide that was supposed to be white, but was dirty from weathering and all of the children who slid on it. He was preparing to catapult himself face-first by rocking back and forth on his tippy toes and heels. "You ready for that new *Spider Man* movie to come out? It looks so dope, right?"

Nave tightened his calf muscles and threw his body forward into the small hole. His smile turned into a panicked scream, "Ohhh shhhh—"

Gideon pursed his lips and shook his head as he made his way to Nave's side. Nave clutched his elbow and tightened his jaw.

White clouds began to travel through the blue sky and block the sunlight. A huge shadow covered the entire playground, though it still looked as orange, black and off-white as a prisoner's jumpsuit. Small honey bees still buzzed with life. The white petals surrounded the yellow disk center of shasta daisies that were in full bloom across the green grass. The weather in Kansas City was in-between summer and fall seasons—perfect.

"Are you okay?"

Gideon quickly kneeled down, his eyes wide and careful as they shifted from one part of Nave's body to another. There was no way he could go back on his promise to their parents: Nave had to come back in one piece, wrapped up in a bow. He hesitated to touch Nave out of fear that he would make worse whatever hurt. So he just put his hand out. Nave grabbed it with his good arm and was pulled to his feet.

"You know, Nave," Gideon started while knocking wood chips off Nave's back. "There's nothing wrong with living outside of the matrix. In real life, heroes don't actually exist, ya know?"

"What are you even talkin about, Gid? I swear, you think you know everything just because you're a senior now."

Nave grimaced while looking at a minor scrape on his elbow. Gideon wasn't paying much attention to him any longer as he looked to the surrounding areas with the full weight of his arm wrapped around Nave's shoulders.

They walked away from the Gregg Klice Community Center playground to the metro bus stop, and though it was

still fairly warm out, a cool wind began to pick-up while the sun was setting. Between the community center and The Black Archives of Mid-America, there was a huge blue, white and yellow baseball mural that read "KC Urban Youth Academy." It wasn't dark yet, but its lights were already illuminating the big baseball field entrance to which it was attached.

"God, you're so annoying." Gideon planted his face in his free hand and shook his head. "This isn't even about me. That hero shit's a myth bro. Like the Easter Bunny, Tooth Fairy and Santa Claus."

Nave's eyes quickly shot open wide as if what Gideon had just said was finally clicking. "Awwwww," Nave crescendoed while covering his mouth with his hand. "I'm telling Mama. You not s'pposed to be saying those type of words, Gideon."

Gideon stopped abruptly in his tracks.

"Oh c'mon Nave, don't be a snitch, bro. You always tryna get me in trouble."

"It's not my fault you be using bad words you know we're both not s'pposed to be using. Maybe your durag is too tight." Nave shrugged and walked on.

Gideon rubbed the top of his head to confirm his durag wasn't indeed "too tight," and rushed in front of Nave. He was prepared to unleash a barrage of insults and physical assaults, but was distracted when Nave looked over his shoulder.

"Hey, look over there! That's KC Superman!" Nave pointed down the sidewalk. "I saw him on TV the other night...Man, he's everywhere."

Before he looked to where Nave was pointing, Gideon flared his nostrils and slapped Nave's finger down.

"What did I tell you about pointin' at strangers, boy? That's how niggas get killed." Gideon slowly turned around and looked in the direction Nave had pointed as a means to avoid the possible fatality of being seen by the person at the end of the finger.

An old black man with a full blue cotton candy beard was posing for a photo with a white dude across the street. They were near the metro stop Gideon and Nave would need to take to get home. Similar to Nave, the black man was wearing a red cape, but he was also wearing sunglasses, a blue Kansas City Royals ball cap, a blue *Superman* t-shirt with "Jesus" hand-stitched across the red "S," and red basketball shorts. Clutched in the black man's arm was a football.

"Aye yo, what is that white dude doin out here?" Gideon pointed with a chuckle.

"You just saw an old black man wearin a *Superman* costume, and that's all you have to say?"

Nave shook his head and threw Gideon's arm down to the ground. "And what happened to not pointing at people? You literally just said we could get killed for that."

Gideon could only chuckle aloud to the sky with his hand on his stomach. Nave folded his arms across his chest.

"Bruh, are you serious? That white dude ain't 'bout to pop nothin off 'round here. Lowkey—nah, scratch that—high-key, he need to stop jeffin and run on back over to Westport before he does something stupid that gets him in trouble. You know white people can't help it..."

While spouting his rhetoric, Gideon's finger slowly pointed back up to the old black man and white dude's direction. This time Nave couldn't help but throw Gideon's arm to the ground, and step in front of his view with his hands on his hips.

"Stop being a racist, Gideon." And with those words, Nave's fiery eyes went watery with fear and anxiety. He knew he had said something that would either get him lectured to death or thrown in a headlock, but instead, Gideon gazed at Nave with concern.

"Nigga, do you even know what being a racist means?"

"W-w-well y-y-yeah," Nave was so frightened about what was to come next he was beginning to stutter. "Miss Griffin told us th-th-that racism is when you say really mean things to—"

"You know what?" Gideon cut off Nave and softly threw his arm around his neck once more with a grin. "Don't even worry bout it, bro. You wanna go take a pic with Supanigga?"

At first, Nave was apprehensive about agreeing to take a picture with "Supanigga" and not "KC Superman," but he eventually mustered enough dignity to nod in agreement.

A jazz musician was blaring a saxophone just outside of the Blue Room while Gideon and Nave crossed the street. A lit sign at the entrance read "Houston Smith, Live!" The smell of barbecue oozed into the sunset. By the time they got to KC Superman, a group of people were saying their goodbyes with hugs, daps, and "God bless yous." Unlike the common panhandler dressed in a superhero get-up, KC Superman didn't seem to be asking for or receiving any payments for his photos or interactions. It was all love and smiles.

"Aye man," Gideon spat out and whipped out his cell phone. "My lil' brother want a photo?"

"Oh, I bet he does," KC Superman leaned back to take in Nave's outfit and grinned wide. His voice was gruff and beaten as if he was getting over a bad summer cold or as if he smoked a pack of cigarettes a day. "With that get-up on, I think I'm the one who should be wanting to take a photo with you, lil' man."

"I saw you on the news the other day. You looked so cool," Nave blurted out. "You're my hero."

Gideon just rolled his eyes and looked around to see if anyone was watching how ridiculous he looked, taking pictures of a grown man in a *Superman* outfit. Nave and KC Superman just continued their conversation, smiling and laughing as if Gideon wasn't even there. At one point, KC Superman stepped to the side of Nave to flex his muscles and curl his arms into his chest as if he were building up chakra.

A gust of wind blew Gideon's attention back to KC Superman and Nave. Gideon didn't notice at first, but KC Superman appeared to be preparing to lift off into the troposphere. KC Superman grunted as his veins bursted out and he looked to the sky.

At first, Gideon just laughed it off. Nave yelled in excitement for KC Superman to take flight, while the wind picked up around them and forced Gideon to doubleback with his eyes lowered in disbelief.

No way. Is Supanigga really 'bout to take off, Gideon thought as the tail of his blue durag levitated. He wasn't certain, but he swore he could see the gravel around them bounce up and down like a California earthquake, and the rumble like a 747 preparing to take off. He stepped forward to assess the situation further, but then an eighteen wheeler barreled by on the street right beside him and forced them all to take a step back.

It was in that moment that Gideon realized the gravel and rumble was likely due to the eighteen wheeler that was about five feet away from crushing them all.

Gideon sighed, and smacked his lips. Man, I knew that shit wasn't real. "Aye are we gonna take this fantasy picture or not, Nave," Gideon's head slouched to the side now. "It's getting late, and I gotta get you home before Mom starts blowin up my phone." '

KC Superman and Nave hurried into their best *Superman* poses. Nave with his signature chest out and his fists on his hips, and KC Superman with his arms flexed to the sky. Both were cheesing as if they had actually just witnessed *Superman* take flight like a bird or a plane. And with the quick flash from the camera on his cell phone, Gideon started making his way towards the metro stop.

"Come on Nave, we gotta get goin. The Metro 'bout to pull up anyway."

Nave looked from Gideon's back to KC Superman. He didn't want to leave just yet, but he knew avoiding trouble with his mom was even more important than speaking with one of his heroes.

"Hey guess what?" KC Superman jumped in the conversation to save the moment. "I'm taking that bus too. We can ride together and chat some more. What do you say?"

Once the bus arrived, Gideon got in line to step on and pulled out his Metrocard.

"Aye don't forget to pull out your card so—" Gideon turned to advise Nave, but was silenced once he saw the two red capes blowing in the wind right behind him.

Nave and KC Superman were going back and forth, pointing out different elements of each other's outfits. Quickly, Nave acknowledged Gideon by holding up his Metrocard to him while continuing to nod his head to KC Superman's comments.

Gideon tapped Nave on the shoulder until he eventually moved closer to him and further away from KC Superman.

"What's up with this homeless dude, Nave?" Gideon whispered. "Is he following us or somethin?"

Nave pursed his lips and rolled his eyes.

"He's not homeless, Gideon," he whispered back in irritation. "And last time I checked, this is public transportation, ain't it?"

"Are ya'll comin on or nah?" The black woman driving the Metro smacked her gum before Gideon had a chance to respond. She looked past Gideon and Nave, and her eyes lit up with life at the sight of KC Superman. "Hey now, Mr. Wheeler is that you? Get in here. What's goin on?"

"Hey there, Rhonda," KC Superman responded. "I'm feelin blessed. How's the drivin today?"

And with that, KC Superman and Nave made their way around Gideon, scanned their Metro cards, and boarded the bus. All Gideon could do was shake his head, grunt to himself, and follow behind them on the bus.

"Good, good." Rhonda the Metro Driver nodded her head with glee as they all stepped on the bus and scanned their cards.

There was an old man in a wheelchair at the front of the bus, and on the opposite side of him, two old women sat beside each other, scoping out everyone and talking up a storm. Not many passengers were in the back, but there were a few folks listening intently to their earbuds or watching people, buildings and pavement go by just outside the stained Metro bus windows.

Once KC Superman, Nave, and Gideon found their respective standing positions on the bus, Gideon leaned into Nave and whispered once more, "Man, why'd you call that dude your hero? I told you heroes aren't real anyways. Besides, you don't even know him."

"Shut up, Gideon" Nave clenched his jaws and turned to Gideon with his fist tightened below his waist and his eyebrows lowered.

And with that, Gideon and Nave reignited their superhero argument, only this time it was more intense as the confined space of the bus elevated their voices even as the bus swayed back and forth while driving on the dirt road. Every now and then, Gideon would notice the few eyes on the bus glaring their direction and tried his best to restrain himself, but couldn't resist the urge to do what he felt was correcting Nave and putting him in his place.

Nave, on the other hand, couldn't help but revel in the heated debate as he knew he could say more to his older brother without being physically punished due to public eyes watching them banter back and forth. Even in his young age, Nave had learned already that no one—not even his parents—would want to be seen as abusive on any level in public. Often, it got him into more trouble once he arrived home, but having his voice be heard every once and awhile was well-worth the beating, especially if it was at the hands of his big brother.

Just when Gideon and Nave could no longer take the verbal exchanges and they were fully prepared to engage in a more physical altercation on the bus, KC Superman stepped in-between the two.

"Hey hey hey now," KC Superman interrupted Gideon and Nave, calm but firm. "There's no sense in two fine young men fighting like this. What's goin on?"

"Why don't you mind your own business, old man?" Gideon snapped. KC Superman stepped in front of Gideon.

"When I see black men committing violence against one another, it becomes my business, young man," KC Superman retorted. Gideon wasn't talking to the light-hearted KC Superman any longer, but Mr. Wheeler. "I suspect your mother and father taught you to respect your elders where respect is due, right son?"

"Ye-yes sir," Gideon's voice was small and shaky, and his eyes filled with embarrassment.

"Now, as I said before..." KC Superman turned to Nave and started with his white teeth shown through a big smile. His voice lightened once more. "What's all the fuss about anyways?"

Nave scrunched up his face and crossed his arms. "He keeps tryna tell me that superheroes aren't real and that everything in the movies isn't real and that I need to take off my cape and grow up. I told him that's not true and he said I'm wrong, but I know I'm right. He's wrong. I just know it—"

Gideon smacked his lips and finally took a stand against Nave. "Man, I'm not wrong and you know it," Gideon said. "You don't see dudes flying around the city saving nobody. All we got is them fake ass superhero movies you keep watching, and people playing dress-up in costumes on street corners. You need to check-in to reality and stop acting so much like a little boy. Grow up. It's okay to be wrong, bro."

"Shut up, you stupid-head! You think you know everything because you're my older brother Gideon, but you don't—"

"Alright alright alright," KC Superman interjected and the boys went quiet. Before speaking again, he took a deep breath of relief and smiled at them both. "Well, I gotta say that this problem you two are dealing with is a great problem to have, compared to what I've experienced in the past...But for starters, watch ya mouth boy, you know better than that."

"Yessir," Gideon muttered while looking away from KC Superman's stern glare.

"The easy part about all this mess is that you're both wrong and you're both right!" KC Superman smiled big to the boys in hopes that this would make them both feel better. Wrong.

"What? No way," Nave shouted aloud, arms flailing.

"Man, you've gotta be kiddin me," Gideon followed, shaking his head. Both folded their arms, unsatisfied with this new mediator's comments.

"Just be patient and listen first," KC Superman tamed, and turned to Gideon. "As the older brother, I can understand you wanting to help your younger brother grow up right in the real world. But you mustn't diminish imagination founded in reality as mere child's play. I mean, do you realize where we are driving through right now?"

Gideon quickly looked out of the bus windows and shook his head. "Well, take a good look because we're in the 18th & Vine Jazz District. Back in the day, this is where all the hip young people used to hang out—from Charlie Parker and Duke Ellington, to Ella Fitzgerald and Buck O'Neil. A lot of you youngins today don't even realize the footprints you're walking behind when you're walking in this area, do ya?"

Again, Gideon shook his head, but no longer were his eyes filled with embarrassment. With KC Superman's words and him pointing out buildings and telling stories of the past while the bus drove out of 18th & Vine, his interest and curiosity had peaked like a child learning of a brand new world.

"I say all that to say, there are heroes all around us. You've heard of the X-Men right?" Gideon hesitated, but nodded his head.

"Man, the X-Men are so cool," Nave blurted out. "Gideon thinks he's a grown up now so he don't know nothin'."

"Shut up, Nave," Gideon nudged. "I do too. I used to watch them growing up...used to couldn't wait till the next one came out."

"Forreal?" Nave's eyes widened, and then lowered in brief bewilderment.

"Well, here's something you both may not know..." KC Superman started.

Gideon and Nave leaned in closer.

"Did you know that Professor X and Magneto were based on Reverend Doctor Martin Luther King Jr. and Brotha Malcolm X?"

"That's crazy." one boy responded.

"Wow, no way," said another.

"Mhmm," KC Superman affirmed with a grin. "So you should never say that heroes don't exist—"

"See! I told you superheroes were real, Gid. In yo face!"

"But," KC Superman cut off Nave's celebration and faced him. "It's equally important to be realistic in our beliefs. The real heroes of this world are people like Dr. King, the Black

Panthers, firefighters, your parents, heck, even your own brother if you really think about it...Enjoy the superhero movies for entertainment, but you have to kill this notion that superheroes actually exist. The only "super" hero to ever walk this fine Earth is Jesus Christ Himself, and you'll be good to know Him if you don't already..."

The boys just stared at KC Superman. They were a bit confused with how they should respond, so they just resolved to say nothing. A few seconds passed and KC Superman cleared his throat, realizing that he might've said too much at once.

"But that's a conversation for another time," KC Superman moved on and began scanning the roads. "Ope! Looks like this is my stop, fellas. Stay safe now. And remember, be nice to each other, ya hear?"

"Yes, sir," Both Gideon and Nave nodded their heads in unison as the bus slowed to an abrupt stop.

KC Superman made his way to the front of the bus. While waving goodbye to Rhonda, he stepped off the bus, his red cape fluttering in the wind behind him.

"Started sounding like grandma at the end, didn't he?" Gideon raised his eyebrows and grinned to Nave.

"Yeeaah," Nave yawned, closed his eyes, and leaned his head against his brother's side. "Almost put me to sleep..."

"Hey, you can't be falling asleep on me like that," Gideon moved over and Nave's head fell a bit before he caught himself. "At least not while we're standing...Here, let's take a seat.

The boys went down in two open seats just behind them. "There's hardly anybody left on this route anyway, and we have another fifteen minutes or so before we get to the house, so we should be coo."

As soon as they sat, Nave snuggled his head on his big brother's shoulder and closed his eyes once again. Gideon could do nothing but smile at how calm and soundless his little brother was now.

"I guess I am kind of excited for that new *Spiderman* movie," Gideon said looking over at Nave's cape. "That mug might be alright after all. Is *Spiderman* your favorite hero,

Nave?"

"Mmm nope." Nave snuggled more on Gideon's shoulder. "It changes every once-in-awhile…"

"Really? Well then, who's your favorite right now? Is it Iron Man or somethin? You know, he seems smart and cool in all those movies, but in the comics he's really just a genius douche. So I hope it's not him, but who's your—"

Gideon glanced down to Nave, who was sound asleep. He gazed outside the bus window at sunset, and smiled at the yellow disk that fell below the horizon of the pink and orange sky.

Helmed from Kansas City, Missouri, R.A. ROGERS is an ambitious storyteller who focuses on contemporary fiction and reflective and experimental poetry. His writing has been published and can be found in many literary and artistic journals including *River City Poetry, Heartland, Rigorous, Flinthills Review, MockingHeart Review, Genre: Urban Arts, Cathexis Northwest Press, Hawai'i Review* and more under the pen name, Ralvell Rogers II. R.A. is currently finishing his debut fiction novel.

Safe:

Tasha Haas

A play in one act

Characters

JENNY, married to Jeff

JEFF, married to Jenny

IRIS, married to Isaac, cat-eye glasses, hipster dress

ISAAC, also a hipster

PIA, Columbian, with a heavy Spanish accent, recently married to Trevor

TREVOR

All are in their late twenties/early thirties.

Tagline: Nothing is more important than being safe.

Synopsis: Three young couples gather for the first time after three years of lockdown while a pandemic swept the world. The government has recently decreed that the virus is here to stay and public health measures, some of which are severe, will be permanent. The couples try to re-establish their friendships while navigating differing opinions about the virus and the unsettling technological solutions to it.

SAFE

Scene 1

(IRIS and ISAAC, bearing potluck dishes and beer, enter JENNY and JEFF'S house)

IRIS: Oh my god. It's you!

JENNY: Oh my god it's you!

(JENNY instinctively moves to hug her, but IRIS steps back. JENNY retreats, standing awkwardly six feet from IRIS. They mime hugging.)

IRIS: I've missed you!

JENNY: I've missed you! You look awesome. New glasses?

IRIS: Meh. (shrugs in reference to the glasses) You cut off all your hair.

JENNY: (flips hair)

I had to do it myself, of course. I think it turned out okay.

IRIS: Definitely. It's so good to see you guys!

(JEFF and ISAAC, also keeping a distance, self-parodying, mime shaking hands and slapping backs. PIA and TREVOR enter, PIA with a bottle of wine.)

EVERYONE but PIA: Heyyyyy!

(Nearly shouting; hyper-enthusiastically. All stand in a circle, unnaturally distanced, self-consciously adjusting their positions incrementally, moving away from one person to find they've moved closer to another on the other side. Nervous laughter as they all notice this. The men and women drift apart into separate circles. The women, stage right, mime talking as the men converse.)

ISAAC: So how the hell are you guys? It's been, like, about a million years.

JEFF: Seems like.

TREVOR: Yeah. Man. And a whole new world.

ISAAC: I literally have not seen anyone but Iris in person in three years.

JEFF: Are you crazy?

ISAAC: Have you?

JEFF: We've seen Jenny's parents, her sister. (adding hurriedly) I mean, we were safe. (laughs) Don't rat us out.

ISAAC: Yeah, that's totally against the law.

JEFF: (staring at ISAAC, the slightest hard edge in his tone) We were safe.

ISAAC: I get it, man, it's hard. It's hard on all of us. I just hope you were. This thing is deadly. And it's not just about you.

JEFF: I said we were safe.

ISAAC: Dude, it's cool. It's great to see you guys. I'm glad we've all made it through. (a beat, a moment of awkward silence)

TREVOR: Nobody likes this. But I guess we have to live with it.

ISAAC: It's the only way we can live. I mean, this is like permanent now. (gestures at their unnatural distance from each other)

JEFF: At least they're letting us get together now. Maybe they'll let up on other restrictions someday too.

ISAAC: Did you hear they're testing personal screens now? They've already been approved in Japan. They reduce transmission by like 15%.

TREVOR: No kidding? That's great news. I still hold out hope I'll get to hug my mom again someday.

JEFF: 15%?

ISAAC: It's better than nothing.

JEFF: Yeah, but at what cost?

TREVOR: Well, that's the question about all of it, isn't it?

ISAAC: Would you rather be dead?

TREVOR: (agreeably, almost clownish, trying to keep the peace) Rhetorical question!

JEFF (focused on Isaac) I mean—how do they work?

ISAAC: Oh—they're minimally invasive. You can still see the other person, and you can hear them, too, almost as good as if there was nothing there although I guess there can be some distortion, maybe an echo. I saw a YouTube about them, they're actually really cool. They literally sterilize the space around you in a 6-foot circumference. And yes (turning to TREVOR), they'll let us hug again.

JEFF: Through plastic?

ISAAC: No, man! They're vibrational. It repels the virus through sound waves or something, It might not feel the same, but you wouldn't know it. It's like a virtual hug but the sensation is real. Just like the sky thing, except they're transparent.

TREVOR: So your mom's hugging an image of your body but not your actual body? How can that be remotely satisfying?

TREVOR: Can we just start drinking beer? Like we used to. How 'bout them Chiefs?

ISAAC: (to Jeff) Think force field.

JEFF: What Chiefs?

TREVOR: Yeah, that's a loss for sure.

(The men pass around beer bottles while trying to maintain 6' apart and avoid touching. ISAAC squirts hand sanitizer from a miniature bottle in his pocket on his hands after taking a bottle from JEFF. They mime drinking and talking, stage left, as the women begin to talk.)

JENNY: So. No baby yet?

IRIS: With the way things are? They won't even deliver you in a hospital now. It's all home births, without a midwife even, and that freaking terrifies me.

JENNY: Well. There are virtual midwives.

(Beat as they all consider this.)

(JENNY starts to reach out to touch PIA's arm, then stops herself, remembering.)

So how was the wedding?

PIA: (shrugs) You know. Small.

IRIS: So were your parents allowed?

PIA: No, but they Zoomed in. The priest too. It was . . . extran'o . . . Honestly, I hated it.

IRIS: But it had to be that way.

PIA: Si, of course. We had to be safe.

JENNY: It's just so sad. So it was just you and Trevor?

PIA: Si. In our dark living room. They wouldn't even let us go into the garden. That was the week they found the virus in rainwater.

IRIS: Oh, yeah, that was terrifying. And it rained all spring. Isaac and I didn't go outside for like months after that.

JENNY: Are you kidding me?

IRIS: What? It wasn't safe.

JENNY: Months?

IRIS: Yeah. Months. We're responsible people. Our neighbors are elderly, our other neighbors had a newborn. It's better than being dead. Or god forbid, killing someone else.

JENNY: It's just hard to believe rain can be that dangerous.

JEFF: (overhearing their conversation, he turns) Are you talking about the rain?

IRIS: Yeah, when they found it in the rain?

JEFF: You know that was based on a flawed study?

ISAAC: What are you talking about? It was fucking NASA that found it.

JEFF: Yeah, NASA later admitted they really had no way to study raindrops on a large enough scale to draw any conclusions. Of course there are going to be DNA fragments of a virus that's been circulating the last three years in the air, the water, everything. That doesn't mean raindrops transmit it. What a bunch of horseshit . . .

IRIS: Jeff. I don't think—

ISAAC: Don't engage with him, honey. He's a virus skeptic.

JEFF: Ha! Name calling now, are we? It was a flawed study. Show me the proof.

(ISAAC and JEFF turn back to their circle and debate silently with vigorous gestures.)

JENNY: Just—whatever. Jeff's very opinionated on this issue. Of course you're right to be careful.

IRIS: And not just for ourselves.

JENNY: Right.

(half-heartedly). It's just— (covers her face with her hands) I'm just— (starts to cry) We've lost so much . . . and how much longer is it going to go on?

(PIA and IRIS exchange worried looks. PIA puts her hand over her heart.)

PIA: I think it's going to be a while, Jenny.

IRIS: Not a while. It's forever. It's permanent. We just have to get used to living like this. At least we can get together now.

JENNY: But concerts! Remember we used to go to concerts? Bars. Parties. Movie theaters. Hugs. The stars, for god's sake. I just want to see the stars again.

IRIS: (looking off-stage, out the imagined window) You can see the stars right now. It's almost dark, they should be on now.

JENNY: The real stars.

IRIS: Well if it keeps us safe, I'm not going to complain.

PIA: (dreamily, with Spanish accent) I remember the stars over the Andes when I was growing up. You don't have stars like that in America, you never have. Billions—trillions, my god, who knows how many stars. And the black, black sky behind them. It looked like a blanket made of black velvet covered with tiny sparkling diamonds. I'll never forget those stars.

JENNY: That sounds amazing. And they're blocked out forever now.

IRIS: Don't be so gloom and doom! We're here, and we're together again. This should be a celebration.

JENNY: (pulling herself together) You're right, Iris. (looking lovingly at IRIS, she hugs herself in place of hugging IRIS) It's so good to see you. Both of you. God, I have so much to tell you.

PIA: Okay, are we drinking, or what? I brought a cabernet from my grandfather's vineyard. (holds up the wine bottle)

JENNY: (reaches in the cabinet for wineglasses; she gets only two) Oh, Columbia must be so beautiful.

PIA: It is. I don't know if I'll ever get to go back.

(JENNY turns on music on her phone; upbeat rock music plays while the women stand in the kitchen. They pour the wine and sip it, Jenny conspicuously declining. Though their dialogue can't be heard, the awkwardness of trying to pour and distribute wineglasses while remaining six feet apart and not touching.)

IRIS: You're not drinking?

JENNY: No, I . . .

IRIS: You're not!

JENNY: (beaming) I am!

IRIS A homebirth? Unassisted? Are you crazy? That's not safe at all.

JENNY (laughing) Calm down, Iris. Jeff says he can do it. He's been watching so many YouTubes, he's practically a doctor by now. And I'm looking for a midwife who will Zoom in; they're out there.

(The women exit stage left. Music fades out.)

JEFF: Hey, let's go outside. I want to show you the deck I built.

ISAAC: You built a deck?

JEFF: (laughs) I had to do something. You can learn anything on YouTube.

TREVOR: Totally. I do our plumbing, carpentry; electrical intimidates me but I'm considering it. It's better than some guy coming in your house and contaminating it . . . (fades out)

(The men exit stage right. A beat, then they return to stage. They stand in the imagined back yard looking up at the sky.)

TREVOR: Pretty clear tonight.

ISAAC: Yeah, not much static tonight. Humidity causes that but they're working on it.

TREVOR: You really can't tell the difference.

JEFF No. You can't tell at all.

(They drink their beers, gazing up, six feet apart.)

CURTAIN

TASHA HAAS is a writer and professor of English at Kansas City Kansas Community College. She has published two collections of short stories: *Certain Dawn, Inevitable Dawn and The Garden of Earthly Delights*. My first book was a finalist for the Thorpe Menn Literary Award, and my fiction has received the Langston Hughes Creative Writing Award. My stories have appeared in *Conjunctions, Stickman Review, South Dakota Review, Flint Hills Review, Coal City Review* and elsewhere.

RALVELL ROGERS, AUTHOR

Interview With An Author:
RALVELL ROGERS
— by Maureen Carroll

Maureen Carroll: Of all of the vehicles available for expression, why do you choose poetry / fiction / non-fiction?

Ralvell Rogers: You know, I don't know exactly why I've been blessed with gifts that pertain to the written and oral traditions. It's really a much bigger question than I think I'm capable of answering, but I do know one of the many goals of those traditions is to help encapsulate moments that would otherwise be lost to human history. I like to think of myself as someone who's simply been chosen to pick up the mantle of the traditions that have been part of history and live on when I'm long gone. Personally, my goal is just to tell the stories I believe to be most overlooked, and yet they're still the most interesting.

MC: How many books (poems) have you written? Which is your favorite?

RR: Oh, I've written hundreds of single poems and more than a few books. Most of them haven't seen the light of day, and only a few probably will. But I think I prefer it that way because once something is published to the world, it's almost as if it no longer belongs to me anymore. Some of my favorite work is stuck in the unpublished archives, which is okay because it's all mine to love, hate and everything in-between. Now, it's important to note that's not my best work. Just my favorite.

MC: What would you say is the most difficult part of writing?

RR: For me? Writing. And reading. It sounds crazy because that's the job, right? To write books and read books, so you can learn how to write more books. The most difficult thing for me is balancing inspiration and procrastination, and then refocusing my attention to actually putting my inspirations on the page.

MC: What does literary success look like to you?

RR: I consider writing an art form, and I think every artist wants to be seen, heard and/or read to a certain extent. That same sentiment applies to me, only I would add that success to me is connecting to the audience I feel I'm attempting to write to and for. If I can do that successfully, then I think all of the other successes will come along with it.

MC Do you view writing as a kind of spiritual practice?

RR: I do. I'm a Bible reader, which means I'm familiar with prophets who expressed God's will through written and oral traditions, amongst many other things. A lot of times I think people view the stories in the Bible as just that—stories. But I believe those stories are much more than that, which means I inevitably believe the spiritual connection between the writers of the Bible and God. I believe many modern writers are in a similar position. They may not be prophets per say, but I know in a lot of my writing, I'll go back years later and wonder did those words really come from me? My mind knows the answer is yes, but my spirit says they actually were bestowed upon me by a higher power. For me, I know that higher power is Jesus.

MC: Who or what turned you on to poetry and writing?

RR: Back when I was studying to get my English degree at Emporia State University, I think I took an intro to poetry course with Kevin Rabas. One of the first assignments he had us write was the "Where I'm From" poetry prompt. By the end of the semester, we ended up writing in a multitude of poetic forms, and I think I was just drawn to the freedom of free verse. No boundaries. No character requirements. Just my thoughts however I could imagine them to be on the page. By the time I graduated from ESU, I had come to learn so much about the relationship between the free expression of poetry and spoken word, and politics and my personal feelings about the state of the world and my position in it. Poetry has always been a very freeing form of expression that I very much enjoy to this day.

MC: Are you originally from Kansas?

RR: Technically, I was born in Kansas City, Kansas, but I would say I'm from Kansas City, Missouri. I have a lot of KCMO pride, so if anyone outside of the City asks, I just tell them I'm from Kansas City, Missouri, to distinguish from KCK, but if you already know the difference, then I'll probably just say Kansas City.

MC: Did you ever consider writing under a pseudonym?

RR: I have. It's mostly to protect myself and my family a bit because of some of the more touchy subjects I find myself dabbling in and out of, but I've always just found pen names to be kind of cool and fun. The mystery of it all is enticing, especially if you're a reader who discovers an author is working under another name.

MC: Do you try to be more original or more traditional as an author?

RR: I think I try to just be me. And wherever that falls, then so be it. I will say that I tend to reflect some of the literary moves that I'm reading at the time or even some of the script writing moves I take note of whenever I catch a movie or show I like.

MC: Do you finish everything you start to write? What happens to old starts?

RR: Absolutely not. It's actually something I've been working on. The relationship I have with a lot of my work is pretty toxic. One day I'm really in love with what I'm coming up with and feel really committed to it, and then the next day, I just let it fall by the waste side. It becomes even more toxic once I get a new story idea. All of a sudden, I'm a cheater.

MC: Do you have any recommendations for young or aspiring writers/poets?

RR: Yeah. If you think you want to be a bestselling author or renowned poet, then fall in love with reading and studying those who are already doing what you do first. And don't compromise your work for the literary business. A lot of writers are out here trying to ride waves and trends because it will greatly impact sales, which is cool if that's what you want to do, but just make certain that it's exactly what you're asking for from yourself. If you want something different—like a writing career more difficult to obtain, but ultimately more rewarding—then do right by yourself and the stories you claim to care so much about.

MC: What are your current projects?

RR: At the moment, I'm working on a couple projects and have been for a few years now. There's something about getting married, being a first-time home buyer, and having kids that just makes one review their lifestyle, their wants and needs, and ultimately who they want to be for themselves and their respective families. I would say I'm definitely in the midst of such a trial right now, but the work I've been trudging through keeps me motivated. My family inspires me to keep going, so making them proud is my #1 goal. One project in particular that I've been putting more of my time into is what I hope will be called the great Kansas City novel. I don't want to jinx it, so I won't share too much, but just know that I'm hoping to highlight Kansas City to the literary world in a way that I think hasn't been done in a very long time.

Helmed from Kansas City, Missouri, R.A. ROGERS is an ambitious storyteller who focuses on contemporary fiction and reflective and experimental poetry. His writing has been published and can be found in many literary and artistic journals including *River City Poetry, Heartland, Rigorous, Flinthills Review, MockingHeart Review, Genre: Urban Arts, Cathexis Northwest Press, Hawai'i Review* and more under the pen name, Ralvell Rogers II. R.A. is currently finishing his debut fiction novel.

Bookstores Carrying *The Write Bridge* Journal

Ad Astra Books & Coffee House, 135 N Santa Fe Ave, Salina KS 67501; 785-833-2235

Claflin Books and Copies, 103 N 4th St, Manhattan, KS 66502; 785-776-3771 claflinbooks.com

Flint Hills Books, 130 W Main · Council Grove, KS 66846; 620-767-5054 flinthillsbooks.com

Middle Ground Books 606 Commercial St, Emporia, KS 66801 785-614-3643 middlegroundbooks.com

Monarch Books & Gifts, 7713 W 151st Street, Overland Park, KS; 913-766-8646 monarchbooksandgifts.com

Prosperos Books & Media, 1800 W 39th St, Kansas City, MO 64111; 816-531-9673 prosperosbookstore.com

The Raven Bookstore, 809 Massachusetts St, Lawrence, KS 66044; 785-749-3300

Red Fern Booksellers, 106 S Santa Fe Ave, Salina, KS 67401; 785-833-2088 redfernbooksellers.com

Rivendell Bookstore, 212 N Broadway St, Abilene, KS 67410; 785-571-5001 ravenbookstore.com

Roundtable Bookstore, 826 N Kansas Ave, Topeka, KS 66608; 785-329-5366 roundtablebookstore.com

Watermark Books & Café, 4701 E Douglas, Wichita, KS 67218; 316-682-1181 watermarkbooks.com

Ask your local bookstore to carry ***The Write Bridge*** Journal!

Thanks To Our Sponsors:

Vern Barnet

Bruce Barlow, Sarah Wallace, and BKB leather

John Bodle, and the Law Office of John Bodle

Iris Craver

D & D Tire, Lawrence, Kansas

Thaddeus Dugan

Kathleen Kaska

Leonard Krishtalka

Bruce Rolfe

Strawberry Hill Museum & Culture Center, KCKS

Barbara Waterman Peters